The Third Room of Preaching

CHURCH OF SWEDEN
Research Series

§

Editor of the series (since 2020): Michael Nausner

1. Göran Gunner, editor, *Vulnerability, Churches and HIV* (2009)
2. Kajsa Ahlstrand and Göran Gunner, editors, *Non-Muslims in Muslim Majority Societies with Focus on the Middle East and Pakistan* (2009)
3. Jonas Ideström, editor, *For the Sake of the World. Swedish Ecclesiology in Dialogue with William T. Cavanaugh* (2010)
4. Göran Gunner and Kjell-Åke Nordquist, *An Unlikely Dilemma. Constructing a Dialogue Between Human Rights and Peace-Building* (2011)
5. Anne-Louise Eriksson, Göran Gunner, and Niclas Blåder, editors, *Exploring a Heritage. Evangelical Lutheran Churches in the North* (2012)
6. Kjell-Åke Nordquist, editor, *Gods and Arms. On Religion and Armed Conflict* (2012)
7. Harald Hegstad, *The Real Church. An Ecclesiology of the Visible* (2013)
8. Carl-Henric Grenholm and Göran Gunner, editors, *Justification in a Post-Christian Society* (2014)
9. Carl-Henric Grenholm and Göran Gunner, editors, *Lutheran Identity and Political Theology* (2014)
10. Sune Fahlgren and Jonas Ideström, editors, *Ecclesiology in the Trenches. Theory and Method Under Construction* (2015)
11. Niclas Blåder, *Lutheran Tradition as Heritage and Tool* (2015)
12. Ulla Schmidt and Harald Askeland, editors, *Church Reform and Leadership of Change* (2016)
13. Kjell-Åke Nordquist, *Reconciliation as Politics. A Concept and its Practice* (2016)
14. Niclas Blåder and Kristina Helgesson Kjellin, editors, *Mending the World? Possibilities and Obstacles for Religion, Church, and Theology* (2017)
15. Tone Stangeland Kaufman, *A New Old Spirituality? A Qualitative Study of Clergy Spirituality in the Nordic Context* (2017)
16. Carl Reinhold Bråkenhielm, *The Study of Science and Religion. Sociological, Theological, and Philosophical Perspectives* (2017)
17. Jonas Ideström and Tone Stangeland Kaufman, editors, *What Really Matters. Scandinavian Perspectives on Ecclesiology and Ethnography* (2018)
18. Dion Forster, Elisabeth Gerle, and Göran Gunner, editors, *Freedom of Religion at Stake. Competing Claims Among Faith Traditions, States, and Persons* (2019)
19. Marianne Gaarden, *The Third Room of Preaching. A New Empirical Approach* (2021)
20. André S. Musskopf, Edith González Bernal and Maurício Rincón Andrade, editors, *Theology and Sexuality, Reproductive Health, and Rights. Latin American Experiences in Participatory Action Research* (2021)

The Third Room of Preaching
A New Empirical Approach

MARIANNE GAARDEN

☙PICKWICK *Publications* • Eugene, Oregon

THE THIRD ROOM OF PREACHING
A New Empirical Approach

Church of Sweden Research Series 19

Copyright © 2021 Marianne Gaarden and Trossamfundet Svenska Kyrkan (Church of Sweden). All rights reserved. Except for brief quotations in critical publications or reviews, no part of this book may be reproduced in any manner without prior written permission from the publisher. Write: Permissions, Wipf and Stock Publishers, 199 W. 8th Ave., Suite 3, Eugene, OR 97401.

Pickwick Publications
An Imprint of Wipf and Stock Publishers
199 W. 8th Ave., Suite 3
Eugene, OR 97401

www.wipfandstock.com

PAPERBACK ISBN: 978-1-7252-7700-7
HARDCOVER ISBN: 978-1-7252-7701-4
EBOOK ISBN: 978-1-7252-7702-1

Cataloguing-in-Publication data:

Names: Gaarden, Marianne.

Title: The third room of preaching : a new empirical approach / by Marianne Gaarden.

Description: Eugene, OR: Pickwick Publications, 2021 | Series: Church of Sweden Research Series | Includes bibliographical references.

Identifiers: ISBN 978-1-7252-7700-7 (paperback) | ISBN 978-1-7252-7701-4 (hardcover) | ISBN 978-1-7252-7702-1 (ebook)

Subjects: LCSH: Preaching | Meaning (Philosophy)

Classification: BV4211.2 G11 2021 (print) | BV4211.2 (ebook)

Updated and slightly revised 2nd edition of *The Third Room of Preaching. The Sermon, the Listener, and the Creation of Meaning.* Louisville, KY: Westminster John Knox Press 2017 (e-book).

Cover picture © Kevin McLaughlin

Scripture quotations from the New Revised Standard Version of the Bible, copyrighted © 1989 by the Division of Christian Education of the National Council of Churches of Christ in the United States of America and are used by permission

Scripture taken from the New King James Version. Copyright © 1982 by Thomas Nelson, Inc. Used by permission. All rights reserved.

Scripture taken from the American Standard Version is in the public domain.

Contents

Preface vii

Introduction ix

1. Empirical Studies and Homiletics 1
2. A Study Report 22
3. Exploring the Third Room in Preaching 55
4. Implications of the Third Room for Preaching 107

Appendix: From Sermon Formation to Preacher Formation 131

Bibliography 151

Preface

THIS BOOK IS THE second, slightly updated and revised edition of *The Third Room of Preaching: The Sermon, the Listener, and the Creation of Meaning*, first published in 2017 (e-book) in the Westminster Homiletics Monographs Series. However, Westminster John Knox Press decided to close the digital series, and the publishing rights were passed on to the Church of Sweden Research Series. I am deeply indebted to researchers Michael Nausner and Jonas Ideström at the Church of Sweden unit for research and analysis for their work adjusting the manuscript to the standards of Wipf and Stock Publishers and thereby making this edition possible.

So, even though this book contains the name of only one author, and although I sometimes felt like a lonely wolf during the process of research and writing, I am indebted to many people. I am standing on the shoulders of homiletical traditions and practices, as well as formulating my empirical homiletics in dialogue with both existing thoughts in my Northern Europe context and in the North American context. My thinking is woven into a network of thoughts with those of many other theologians. In short, this book would never have been possible without the support of many people.

First and foremost, I thank the generous churchgoers who in the interviews so honestly shared their personal experience of the worship services and the sermons, and who let me have a glimpse into their private lives of faith. I equally have to thank the participating preachers for fruitful cooperation and for willingness to let me have an insight into their sermon preparation and theological considerations. Without churchgoers and preachers who offered generous, frank and open interviews, the contents of this book would never have been possible.

Furthermore, some people need special thanks. I am deeply indebted to the North American professor of Preaching Ronald J. Allen. Ron has been invaluable resource during the entire editorial work with his

Preface

constructive feedback, guidance and language assistance (which has given him cheap laughs and many extra working hours because of my Danish-English spelling). I also give thanks to the Danish professor of Sociology Peter Gundelach, whose invaluable professional support has made it possible to navigate in methodical foreign waters. Professor Marlene Ringgaard Lorensen and Pastor Pia Nordin Christensen are my dear homiletical colleagues and friends in Denmark, and during the years of this project, they have been great sparring partners, especially taking the edge off my sometimes overly bombastic statements. And last but not least, I am indebted to my beloved husband, Michael for having patience and heart space, for being a persistent coach and cheerleader, and for offering food service during the process of preparing this book.

Many pastoral seminary students and clerics have been critical and constructive voices before, during and after the working process with both the empirical investigation and the results presented in this book. These interactions have given rise to theological reflections, intense discussions, and vigorous response. I hope this book will serve as continuing inspiration and as an invitation to further homiletical reflection and discussions about how to preach and how to help students learn to preach.

Marianne Gaarden
Bishop's residence, Nykøbing Falster, Denmark, May 2021

Introduction

THEOLOGIANS THESE DAYS TYPICALLY begin with a description of their social and theological locations. I follow that custom by outlining my perspective for this book. I have worked as a Danish pastor as well as a teacher and researcher of homiletics and now I serve as a bishop in the Danish Lutheran church. My perspective is that of both the preacher in the pulpit and the congregation in the pews of the Danish Lutheran Church. I have conducted empirical research into preaching in the Danish context, and I shall present this data and analyze it in dialogue with other international empirical surveys from primarily the Nordic countries and North America. I shall draw out connections among these bodies of data and to insights and discoveries that point to a "a third room" in which preaching takes place, a new dimension in understanding what happens in sermons from the perspectives of both preacher and listeners.

As a newly ordained pastor, I preached one of my first sermons for a congregation of over 1,200 people on Christmas Eve. I was quite nervous and had worked very hard to prepare a sermon in accordance with the listener-centered approach that I had learned from studying rhetoric and the New Homiletic of "narrative" sermons. Instead of explaining my theological point—that the true way to Christian joy is to forget rather than satisfy oneself—I tried to reveal it by using an anecdote from real life. A 36-year-old Danish woman had visited a female doctor to renew her prescription for contraception. The doctor, with an ethnic background from the Middle East, told her: "Oh, you Danes are so self-centered; you have not learned to ignore your own needs in favor of another person's, and no one can teach you so well as your own *baby*." A few days later, I received an e-mail from a man in the congregation who thanked me for the sermon. I was proud and grateful, until I read the last lines, in which he explained *why* he liked the sermon so much: he was against contraception too![1]

Introduction

Like most preachers I learned right from my first days of preaching that listeners take elements of the sermon and build them into their own pre-understanding, which is often inconsistent with the preacher's intention. Listeners may even comment on something they have heard in the sermon, which the preacher knows for sure that he or she did not say. If we focus on the preachers' perspective, we can blame the listeners for failing to understand our way of thinking. Perhaps the listener did not pay close enough attention. As preachers, we often assume it is possible to transfer our perspectives on the Bible, theology, and ethics to our listeners, as if meaning can be transferred from one consciousness to another. This is called the "transfer model" of communication.

However, since Ludwig Wittgenstein's statement that words have no isolated meaning in themselves but get their meaning primarily from how words are used in a *context*, the traditional notion of communication as a one-way transfer from an active speaker to passive listeners has been euthanized and deconstructed several times. Yet in practice, the transfer model continues to be quite resistant. It pops up everywhere in contemporary homiletics—probably because of the lack of an alternative communication model or a communication theology to explain fully the preaching "event." This transfer of communication paradigm is persistent and hard to overcome in practice.

Throughout history, preaching has been studied through the lens of theology, Biblical text analysis, Church history or dogmas, according to the preacher's theological family, and interpretation of the gospel. Most writers in homiletic discourse take for granted that the preachers' role is to provide the congregation with an understanding of the gospel at a semantic and cognitive level. By transferring perspective from the mind of the preacher to the mindsets of the congregation, the preacher hopes to provide the congregation with direct, propositional answers to questions such as these: Who is God, and what does God offer and require of us in this complex world of joy and suffering? How can the preacher proclaim the "good news" in the midst of the most dreadful experiences in life? The preacher seeks for words as instruments for creating a specific understanding.

Qualitative empirical research into the sermon-listening process conducted in Denmark, other European countries, and the United States is challenging some of the most accepted homiletic axioms, especially concerning the transfer model of preaching. This research first challenges the assumption that listeners simply absorb what the preacher says in a

Introduction

one-to-one intellectual way. This perspective is too limited a way of interpreting what happens in listeners when they receive the sermon. From the perspective of the pew, the preaching event is not primarily a question of the listeners' transferring the preachers' understandings to their own *understanding*; rather, what happens when listeners hear the sermon is that they *create meaning*—or to use a theological word—the sermon becomes an "incarnation" of meaning in which both preacher and congregation are stakeholders. The encounter between the preachers' outer words and the listeners' inner experience brings about what I call a *Third Room* in which the listeners, in internal dialogue, create a surplus of meaning that was previously not present in either the preacher's intent or the listener's frame of reference.

From this point of view, semantic meaning is not embedded solely in the preacher's words or in the frame of listening the listener brings to the sermon but is *emergent* in the shared situation. The preacher cannot control the production of meaning in the mind, heart, and life of the listener but must surrender those possibilities to the preaching event and to what happens in the Third Room. The preacher is not the carpenter who builds the Third Room, yet the Third Room is dependent on the preachers' willingness to participate in the construction of the Third Room as a tool. Preachers are not *holding* the tool but are the tool to *be held* by the "real carpenter of the Third Room," namely: God. With this understanding of God, preachers are participating in God, and whether they serve as a tool in the preaching event, depends upon their willingness to relinquish themselves to God. This new concept opens a fresh homiletic paradigm that raises a burst of new questions:

- How are we to understand the Third Room?
- Who builds it?
- What happens in it?
- Where can we find it?
- What does it contain?
- How can the preacher create it?
- Is the sermon intrinsically different from any other spoken form of address, such as the political speech, the conference lecture, or the funeral eulogy?

Introduction

- Or can the Third Room emerge in these speech acts as well? Is the Third Room bracketing the role of God?
- Or what is the role of the Holy Spirit in the Third Room?
- What does the presence of this Third Room mean for the way preaching is taught?

This book introduces and develops the notion of *The Third Room of Preaching*.

The idea of this Third Room grew inductively out of my empirical research, in dialogue with the work of other researches, into the preaching event that utilizes qualitative interviews with both preachers and listeners as analyzed through "grounded theory." The interviews were carried out in in various Danish churches and provided the basic material for my PhD dissertation in 2014.[1] The goal of my work is to generate a grounded theory of the preaching event in order to add an empirical approach to the discussion of how to preach in the 21st century. By using empirical methods adapted from the social sciences, I hope to bring the new perspectives into the ongoing discussion of contemporary scholarship in preaching by providing information on how listeners interact with and create meaning when hearing the sermon. More broadly, I hope to show how empirical and theological approaches collaboratively can enrich our theological understanding of preaching.

The motivation and inspiration for the study grew out of tension that I began to perceive between the listener-centered approach to preaching (embedded in contemporary North American and European homiletics) and my own observations that there is a discrepancy between the academic theology of preaching and ordinary people's *experience* of preaching. The literature of preaching commended the sermon as a transfer of information, perspective or feeling, but I found that listeners often came away from the sermon with something other than what the preacher intended. This raised the question, "How do listeners actually listen to sermons?"

Exploring this network of answers to the question opens up additional questions. Embedded in contemporary homiletic theories are

---

1. The dissertation defended at Aarhus University was entitled: *The Emerging Sermon. A Qualitative Research into the Words of the Preacher and the Situated Listener in Worship* [Den emergente prædiken: En kvalitativ undersøgelse af mødet mellem prædikantens ord og den situerede kirkegænger i gudstjenesten] (2014). In addition to the results of my own research, I will cite several other contemporary empirical research projects in the Nordic countries.

INTRODUCTION

sub-assumptions about the listening process, which I will illuminate with empirical discoveries from the perspective of the pew.[2] Embedded in contemporary homiletic theories are sub-assumptions about the listening process, which I will illuminate with empirical discoveries from the perspective of the pew. For instance regarding the preachers' role as a tour guide being able to lead the listeners through the same tour as the preacher has traveled, implies that listeners travel in the same country of experiences as the tour guide.[3] Regarding the preachers' role as a moviemaker being able to form the listeners' consciousness by means of images, implies that the preacher knows the listeners private experiences, and can govern the associations activated by the images.[4] Or by shaping the sermon in a specific way the preacher should be able to form faith quite differently from a sermon shaped another way.[5] "If the sermon does obey the rhetorical rules and is shaped according to the hearers' patterns of listening, then it will connect to the hearers and communicate more successfully."[6] Thus, homileticians assumed that the listeners' reception and faith can be controlled and managed. However, these sub-assumptions are typically based on a theoretical understanding and then applied to interpreting the listener's experience. The traffic thus travels one way across the bridge of interpretation—and the theory is used to explain what happens when people listen. But the researcher seldom travels the *other* way across the bridge, to attend to what actually happens from the perspective of the listener. If faith also comes from listening, why not listen to those who listen?

The book contains four chapters and an appendix. Chapter One describes empirical studies in North European and North American homiletic literature, and the challenge of formulating a contemporary communication theology. Chapter Two is a study report containing the theoretical, epistemological, and methodological basis for the research and a presentation of how the inductive working process led to the notion of the Third Room. Chapter Three describes what happens in the Third Room and illustrates how listeners create meaning through interaction with the

---

2. At the time, I wrote the monograph I was teaching homiletics at the Pastoral Institute in Aarhus and was using literature primarily from the new homiletic.

3. As argued by Fred B. Craddock in *As One Without Authority*.

4. As argued by David Buttrick in *Homiletic* or Eugene L. Lowry in *The Homiletical Plot*.

5. As argued by Thomas G. Long in *The Witness of Preaching*.

6. Long. "And How Shall They Hear?" 177.

Introduction

preacher as conversation partner. Chapter Four focuses on the implication for the preacher as the co-builder of the Third Room. The Appendix contains a suggestion for new work on the pedagogics of expanding the idea of the Third Room into the training and forming of preachers, which is a move from sermon formation towards preacher formation.

1

Empirical Studies in Homiletics

THIS CHAPTER GIVES A description of empirical studies in practical theology and sums up the arguments for using empirical research within the field of homiletics. Such research is being undertaken in certain theological schools in North America. I shall then turn to the empirical studies in Northern European homiletic literature and include a short description of the national churches in the Nordic countries, as there are notable ecclesial differences from the North American context.[1] Finally, I will compare the homiletic literature from the two contexts and define some of the challenges when formulating a contemporary communication theology adequate for preaching today.

1.1 EMPIRICAL STUDIES IN PRACTICAL THEOLOGY

In recent years, the *empirical turn* to gain insight and knowledge into the *practice* of faith has grown exponentially in practical theology.[2] The em-

---

1. I use the term "Nordic" because it includes Iceland, Greenland, Finland, Denmark, Sweden, and Norway, plus the territories of the Faroe Islands. In the past, the term "Scandinavia" was limited to Denmark, Sweden, and Norway, but now generally includes Finland and Iceland.

2. For an international overview of the accretion of empirical research in practical theology—in some circles named Ethnography—see for example Ward, *Perspectives on Ecclesiology and Ethnography;* Scharen, *Explorations in Ecclesiology and Ethnography;* Scharen and Vigen, *Ethnography as Christian Theology and Ethics.* In addition, the *Journal of Ecclesial Practices* has published many articles which have contributed to shaping this young field of study. Furthermore, the Ecclesiology and Ethnography network and the Ecclesial Practices Group at the American Academy of Religion (AAR) has contributed to this new development.

pirical turn has encouraged comprehensive research into the practice in organized and individual forms of Christian life. Empirical research within theology is concerned with how theology can be understood in *praxis*—as theory formed in practice.[3] This international development is seen as a part of a wider *practical* approach to theology, just as the practical development in social sciences within the last five to six decades. The researcher seeks to understand what really happens in participants in religious practice from the standpoint of what the participants really report rather than assuming that a pre-formed theory will explain what happens.

However, besides a richer understanding of the praxis of the Christian life, bringing empirical method into theology entails a conviction that theological reflection is not separated from the actual practice of faith, but is embedded in it. This book conceives of empirical research in theology as an integral part of the normative enterprise in theology.[4] It contradicts the assumption that the normative dimension of theology is located in the idealistic and rational mind, and that cognition is separate from the immanent and social world. The results of empirical research within the ecclesial practice of faith are therefore a source for theological reflection, in line with sources from church history and theological literature.

Empirical research is playing an increasingly important role in theology in general and in practical theology in particular. Even exegesis operates with an empirical approach, due to the inspiration from contemporary literary theory, and especially the reader-response criticism, a school of literary theory focusing on the reader's or listener's experience of a literary work and their role in creating meaning.[5] The reader-response theory recognizes

---

3. Empirical research as present in this book can easily be categorized and criticized for taking a liberal theological position, because empirical research takes into account the roles of inner words/dialogues for individual meaning making in the practice of preaching. However, empirical research is not identical with liberal theology.

4. This is a delicate issue as the relationship between already established normative dogmatic theology and empirical research has often been, as Natalie Wigg-Stevenson describes it: "Rather, the problem relates to the particular way of configuring the relationship between typically normative theological sources and the theological descriptions of practice. Dogma and description are pitted against each other in a competition, with dogma's victory decided before the match even begins. But when we allow pre-established dogmatic criteria to trump the descriptions of practice that do not quite fit our idealized vision, then those descriptions are at best, reduced to the theological construction at hand. Ethnographic theology therefore needs to challenge and reshape traditional theological normativity rather than endeavor to reproduce it" ("From Proclamation to Conversation").

5. Contemporary reader-response criticism began in the 1960s and 1970s, particularly

the reader as an active agent who imparts "real existence" to the work and completes its meaning through interpretation. Reader-response criticism argues that literature should be viewed as a performing art in which each reader creates his or her own, possibly unique, text-related performance. The framing questions of interpretation are transformed from "What does this text mean?" to "What can this text do?"

Along with the transfer of "meaning" from the author's intention to the reader's interaction with the biblical books, a new hermeneutic emerged.[6] The Danish biblical exegete, Gitte Buch-Hansen describes a key distinction that has emerged in exegesis: the historical *world behind the text*, the literary and rhetorical *world within the text* and the social and cultural *world in front of the text*.[7] The three different exegetical paradigms are echoing three different roles of the preacher operative in contemporary scholarship in preaching.

If the accent is upon the world *behind* the text, the preacher is in the role of expert or the "herald," as described by Karl Barth and his successors in dialectical theology. The task of preaching is to point to the *keryx* (or message) of the Holy Scripture which bears witness to revelation.[8] If the accent is upon the world *within* the text, the text is separated from its context, and the preacher is in the role of poet or storyteller, creating a new meaning within the text, as suggested by Fred Craddock and his

---

in the US and Germany, on the initiative of Fish et al., *Mark and Method*.

6. Ernst Fuchs and Gerhard Ebeling were innovators of the approach to the New Testament known as the "New Hermeneutic," which focuses on how contemporary listeners interact with the biblical text. The New Hermeneutic is based on the presupposition of the timelessness of the text and claims that this timelessness necessarily means that it holds new meaning for each new reader. In this way, the New Hermeneutics is inspired by reader-response criticism. This timelessness means that the meaning of the text is not bound to the original historical context. The New Hermeneutic also recognizes that all translation between languages implies imprecision due to the different semantic meanings in given languages. Translations to new languages will inherently give rise to new understandings or perspectives on a given text. Both Fuchs and Ebling insist on the text's practical relevance for the world in front of the biblical text of today, and they were occupied with the question of how the language of the Bible strikes, impacts, or touches contemporary listeners.

The North American homiletician, Dawn Ottoni-Wilhelm accounts for the relationship between the New Hermeneutic and the New Homiletic in "New Hermeneutic, New Homiletic, and New Directions."

7. Gitte Buch-Hansen is Professor of New Testament Studies at Copenhagen University. See Buch-Hansen and Poulsen, *Biblen i gudstjenesten*, 13–41.

8. Barth, *Homiletics*, 71–75.

colleagues in the New Homiletic.[9] If the accent is upon the world *in front of* the text, the preacher is in role of pastoral care, inviting the congregation to create their own meaning in dialogue with the text. Listeners are seen as alienated in their otherness, connoting Other-wise preaching. "Otherwise" preaching is a concept invented by John McClure in his *Other-wise Preaching: A Postmodern Ethic for Homiletics*, but created in dialogue with other homiletician.[10] This homiletical movement, inspired by French philosopher, Emmanuel Lévinas, emphasizes the decentering influence of words of "others" and the listeners' co-authorship of preaching. Other-wise preaching has moved away from an ideological, abstract philosophy towards a more pragmatic, embodied approach to homiletics. It challenges the traditional perception of preaching, not only as one-way communication. Having rejected the traditional transfer-model of communication, other-wise homileticians are searching for an alternative model of communication.[11] The three different exegetical paradigms are not to be seen as alternatives—but in practice often overlap each other.

1.2 THE ARGUMENT FOR EMPIRICAL STUDIES IN PRACTICAL THEOLOGY

Although empirical research has grown increasingly in practical theology and has even paved its way into exegesis at the beginning of the new millennium, the implementation of empirical methods in the field of homiletics has not as yet had the same influence either internationally or in the United States.[12] From a Danish perspective, North American homiletics is remarkably influenced by the philosophical tradition that originated in United States as a pragmatic approach to preaching.[13] In general "what works"

---

9. For preaching as storytelling see Craddock, *As One without Authority* and *Craddock on the Craft of Preaching*. For overviews see Eslinger, *Web of Preaching* and Allen, *Patterns of Preaching*.

10. McClure, *Other-wise Preaching*; Allen, *Preaching and the Other*.

11. McClure, "What I Now Think," 98–99.

12. For an overview of overview Anglican, German and Dutch speaking empirical homiletic studies up to 2013 see Rietveld, "Survey of the Phenomenological Research." For a South Korean survey see Park and Wepener, "Empirical Research."

13. Developed in the nineteenth century by Charles Sanders Peirce and with the contributors William James and John Dewey in the twentieth century. The philosophy of pragmatism "emphasizes the practical application of ideas by acting on them to actually test them in human experiences." Pragmatism focuses on a "changing universe rather than an unchanging one as the Idealists, Realists and Thomists had claimed." See Gutek,

counts! Taking this into account it is quite surprising that North American homiletics has not implemented empirical methods more broadly. In Northern Europe, influenced by a philosophical idealism that originated in Europe,[14] it is necessary in some theological contexts to argue for the empirical approach to theology.

The obviously useful insight gained from the empirical methods has disarmed the critical voices of implementing empirical methods into practical theology. However, this international empirical turn within Practical Theology, taking place within North America as well, tends to evoke a theological resistance in certain theological schools influenced by Barthian ways of thinking (as in some post-liberal circles and some evangelical camps), similar to Northern European theologies being influenced by dialectical theology. Thus, theological voices have expressed criticism at the appearance of empirical theology. The critique can, for example, be like this:

> My account renders empirical theology and its method unsatisfying in several important ways: 1) metaphysically, it undercuts foundations; 2) religiously, it omits the universality and eternity of theological truths; 3) historically, in emphasizing the speculative and diminishing the evidentiary.[15]

To evaluate this criticism let me briefly summarize the main arguments *for* the use of empirical methods in practical theology in general and homiletics in particular. The above criticism assumes that Christianity is an ahistorical, universal and metaphysical truth to which theology has privileged access. Of course, theology, thereby stands in opposition to empirical research with its situational, contextual, and anthropocentric approach. However, from the perspective of using empirical methodology in

---

Philosophical, Ideological, and Theoretical Perspectives, 76–100. Pragmatism rejects the idea that the function of thought is to describe, represent, or mirror reality. Instead, pragmatists consider thought an instrument or tool for prediction, problem solving, and action. Pragmatists contend that most philosophical topics—such as the nature of knowledge, language, concepts, meaning, belief, and science—are all-best viewed in terms of their practical uses and successes.

14. The philosophical tradition of idealism, which dominated the nineteenth-century philosophy, emphasized the mental or "ideal" character of all phenomena. Idealism asserts that reality, or reality as we can know it, is fundamentally mental, mentally constructed or otherwise immaterial. The philosophy was founded and developed by European idealists such as Immanuel Kant, G. W. F. Hegel, Johann Gottlieb Fichte, Friedrich Wilhelm Joseph Schelling, and Arthur Schopenhauer.

15. Dean, "Empirical Theology." Dean was Professor of Religion at Gustavus Adolphus College, Minnesota.

theological reflection, the primary question is whether the epistemological *starting point*, is a trustworthy starting point for (and continuing partner in) theological reflection.

The criticism claims that the main problem is that the methods of social science and theological reflection are governed by entirely different paradigms.[16] This point of view implies that there is an unbridgeable gap between the empirical and theological approaches to interpretation. For critical voices, theology is understood as a *sui generis* concept, incomparable to all other concepts, as theology is engaged in the transcendent reality independent and separate from our human immanent and limited understanding of that transcendent reality. This logic entails a theological conviction that there is *a priori* no point of contact between human and God. Therefore, there should be an unbridgeable gap or a dichotomy between an anthropocentric and a theocentric perspective.

However, I join others in questioning the premise of thinking that theology has a privileged access to transcendent reality through revelation independent of immanent manifestation. The distinction between an anthropocentric and a theocentric perspective easily leads to the false assumption that the believer has a privileged access to an objective truth about God irrespective of their own participation in obtaining this truth. The fault of this theological thinking is its blindness to the epistemological starting point: that theological discourse is always bound to human reasoning. Indeed, all human awareness contains interpretive elements that arise from context. In acknowledging our own participation in doing theology, the search for independent or external truth breaks down.

Theology is a human enterprise and, as such, is always situational, bound to time and context, governed by own personal preconceptions and theological agenda. Therefore, the truth—also the revealed truth in the Bible—is only granted us in terms of interpretation. The epistemological starting point for the empirical methods inspired from social science is not different from the epistemological starting point for doing theology. Therefore, it is a false distinction to assert that empirical studies and practical theology are governed by different paradigms.

This does not imply a rejection of the experience of transcendence as an ahistorical, universal and eternal truth, but such experience is fundamentally immanent, due to our awareness of our immanent nature and

---

16. Ganzevoort, "Van der Ven's Empirical/Practical Theology," 53–74. Ganzevoort is Professor of Practical Theology at Vrije University.

limited cognition.[17] The concept of transcendence is rather a concept of the *experience of transcendence*, I shall argue, as we have no other access to the transcendent. Empirically, the experience of transcendence is a fact, and it happens in the immanence—in the world that is immediately given.[18] This moves the ontological question of who God is to *where God happens*. It does not imply, that unless God "happens," God does not exist, but it implies a rejection of the discourse of the transcendent, independently of our immanent nature, as the immanent human always is participating. This approach to transcendence emphasizes human experience, which is precisely the focus of qualitative research.

1.3 EMPIRICAL STUDIES IN NORTH EUROPEAN HOMILETICS

The Nordic "Folk Churches" are commonly referred to as Lutheran "state churches." The Evangelical Lutheran Churches in the North of Europe are literally named the "folk church" in the Scandinavian languages.[19] Despite the name it is *not* referring to more informal communities less tied to institutions. A folk church in a Nordic ecclesial context is from a North American perspective a "state church." The notion of the *folk church* in the Scandinavian countries has been a central part of the self-understanding of the Nordic Lutheran majority churches over the last hundred years and the folk church is explicitly built into the Danish Constitution, unchanged since 1849.[20] The folk church has been a national ethnic church in Denmark building on the state church, which preceded it. The Nordic ecclesial contexts have certain characteristics, due to the historical role of churches in the Nordic societies. One of these characteristics is the strong influence of Lutheran folk churches, which have shaped the Nordic societies and the various forms of the folk church. In contrast to a North American ecclesial context, these Nordic societies, building on the Evangelical-Lutheran

---

17. I will return to the question of how to define "experience" in ch. 2.

18. I am indebted to Dorthe Jørgensen, a Danish professor of philosophy for her work on philosophical aesthetics. She has developed a modern metaphysics of experience and emphasizes the experience of transcendence as the experience of a surplus of meaning. See, for example, Jørgensen, "Experience of Immanent Transcendence."

19. For an explanation of the Nordic Folk Churces see, for instance, Ryman and Lodberg, *Nordic Folk Churches*.

20. The Danish word for folk church is "folkekirke." The definition of the folk church has no equivalent elsewhere in the world and cannot be applied in English context. It belongs to German and the Nordic languages.

tradition, used to be homogeneous with close ties between church and state.[21] In spite of that—or some might even argue, *because* of that—the Nordic countries are now among the most secular in the world.[22]

From a North American perspective, it is odd, and maybe unintelligible, that around 77% of the Danish population are members of the Danish Lutheran Church. They pay Church tax of around 0.9% of their annual incomes, but only around 2% of these members regularly attend worship. The members primarily use the folk church in relation to the religious ceremonies of baptism, confirmation, marriage, and funeral. Consequently, congregational attendance is more erratic and volatile—less so in rural areas. These things are more so in urban areas, in which people in the pew can be different from Sunday to Sunday. Because of the religious reserve of Danish people anyone can come to church, sit in the pew, sing the hymns, pray the prayers, listen to the sermon – and then leave church without speaking to anyone. This form of worship and congregational life differs considerably from that of North America and is an important background for the empirical research presented in the book. Many participants do not sense themselves as being an inherent part of a congregation. By contrast, Christians in North America feel that they are much more a part of an ecclesial community.[23]

Although many denominations exist in the Nordic countries, the vast majority of Christians are members of the *national* Church. On the other hand, *within* the national churches there are quite different theologies in play, since there is no real consensus about what the folk church actually means. On a more popular level the folk church often designates a majority church with "low threshold" which is open to everyone and does not ask too much of its members in terms of active engagement and articulated faith.[24]

---

21. In 2000 the folk church separated from the state in Sweden and the same development took place in Norway in 2012. In Denmark the folk church and state are still intertwined, but this relationship is politically debated.

22. For a historical mapping of the folk churches in the Nordic countries see Eriksson et al., *Exploring a Heritage*.

23. This can be one of the reasons why the Australian homiletician, David Rietveld, reading an article presenting some of the results of my dissertation, points to the "Lack of appreciation of how sensing being part of a congregation influences listeners" in Rietvelt, "Survey of the Phenomenological Research of Listening," 42.

24. Fagermoen, "Ecclesiology and Ethics."

One might think that an empirical survey of a folk church in a small Nordic country like Denmark is not relevant for other than Danes or other Nordic peoples. However, although data is generated and analyzed—and I as a researcher am situated in a Danish ecclesial context—I have discovered through my participation in international homiletic discourse that the findings of our Nordic studies transcends the cultural and ecclesial differences between the Nordic countries and the North America context. One of the reasons is probably that the goal of the methodology I used, Grounded Theory, is *conceptualization*, and not investigation of a specific group, like Danish congregations' sermon reception. The new concepts—in this case the Third Room of Preaching—is extracted from categories and the characteristics associated with those categories formed by systematic analysis. In accordance with the premise of doing Grounded Theory the result is not to be considered as an objective truth. Rather the results are to be judged by the reader by means of the following four criteria: *fit, relevance, workability,* and *modifiability.*

The responses so far have often been that the result intuitively fit preachers' experiences, such as: "Yes, this is exactly the way it is, and it has been regarded as highly relevant for the practice of preaching." According to workability it seems on one hand to be a bigger challenge to preach as the preachers have to use them self in a more personal way; on the other hand it has been received as a great relief for the preacher realizing they do not possess such a power to control the listeners production of meaning. In relation to modifiability, e.g., a Norwegian group of researchers has elaborated and modified the notion of the Third Room.[25] Thus, it is my hope that the empirical results can be a useful voice in the international homiletic discourse exploring the preaching event.

Until recently there has been a very limited theological tradition in the Nordic countries on which to build homiletic theory based in research into actual practice. However, there is a rapidly growing interest in applying empirical methods to practical theology for the benefit of theological reflection as well as for the practice of ministry.[26] In this respect, the Nordic context follows international trends in the new millennium towards qualitative empirical research—often named ethnographically oriented research—in the field of ecclesiology.

---

25. In ch. 2, these four criteria will be explained further.

26. For an overview of the trends see Kaufman, "Mapping the Landscape of Nordic Research."

The Third Room of Preaching

Although theologians of practical theology were already using the term, "the empirical turn" in the late 1960s, it did not then refer to the practical and concrete use of empirical methods, but to a theoretically founded knowledge about practices implemented from other professions and disciplines. The homiletical literature of the time drew upon philosophy of language, the linguistic turn, rhetorical theory etc. Not until recently have theologians considered using social science qualitative methodology in *theology*. Implementing new methods, however, offers new perspectives, which in turn may affect and broaden the understanding of practical theology and, of course, homiletics too.

As qualitative research investigates reality as experienced by human beings, the methodology presupposes room for *experience* in theology. In contexts influenced by a dialectical theology that perceives human beings as "sinners," there has been a widespread suspicion of human experience. From that point of view, there is no such a thing as a point of contact between God and human.[27] Human experiences are at best irrelevant and at worst harmful to theology.

The problem with such a massive rejection of the human dimension in doing theology lies in its blindness to the epistemological starting point: There is no knowledge without someone who knows in a particular way, so also theological knowledge is a matter of perspective.[28]

Throughout history the theology of preaching has principally been formulated by well-educated and theologically trained, primarily Eurocentric men, based on their studies of biblical texts, church history, and the theology of previous theologians, but seldom based on lay people's ordinary faith experience. The central paradigm has been that the theology of preaching is rooted in thinking and thinking and experience have often traditionally been seen as separate and incompatible categories.[29] Theology has been seen in relation to an objective text, and experience in relation to a subjective individual. So, it is necessary to argue for the *empirical* approach to homiletics, and especially for the contribution to theological statements.

---

27. Barth argues that there is no such thing as an anthropocentric point of contact ("Anknüpfungspunkt") between human beings and God. Barth, "Nein. Antwort an Emil Brunner," 62.

28. I will return to the epistemological starting point in the study report in ch. 2.

29. The dichotomy can be traced back to the foundation of ancient Greek philosophy where the Aristotelian concept that material reality is inconsistent with the Platonic vision of the idealistic world.

The first orientation towards empirical research in Northern Europe began in Germany and the Netherlands in the late 1970s and the beginning of the 1980s.[30] The common approach for these first surveys was theoretically inspired by studies in mass media on the assumption that it is possible to "break through" into the listeners' consciousnesses with a message; misunderstandings are mere hindrances to be eliminated. Central to this understanding of communication as the transference of information is the attempt to reduce "noise" in order to let the information arrive in as undisturbed a manner as possible.[31]

At their ordination, ministers in Nordic folk churches sign an oath of office declaring that they will strive "to preach the gospel clean and pure." It has often been interpreted as if the gospel can be formulated and communicated in a way completely independent of cultural formation and completely independently of interpretive elements. It is understandable if the words in the vow embody an inherent approach to preaching in which communication is reduced to a matter of transferring information from the Bible to the congregation. From this perspective, the practice of preaching appears as a monological one-way communication from an active sender to passive receivers.

The German surveys were primarily designed to investigate and assess the impact and effect of the sermon and analyze it in dialogue with the preacher's intention. Did the congregation hear the sermon in accordance with the preacher's intention? The implied communication theory assumed that effective communication could transfer meaning from an *active* speaker to a *passive* receiver. Of course, the listener was not perceived as passive, but the researchers showed no awareness of the activity of the listener participating in the preaching event. However, the results indicated that the listeners did not only passively overtake the sermon: rather they actively interpreted and transformed the message into their own situation in accordance with their own interests and pre-understanding. There was a tendency to regard these results as hindrances and hurdles in preaching which should be overcome by greater rhetorical effort. Preachers would have to communicate more precisely in order to make the congregation understand the message correctly. Mischievously, we might ask if the carpenter from Nazareth 2000 years ago should also have communicated his

---

30. See for example Piper, *Predigtanalysen*; Grandthyll, *Die Wirkung der Predigt*; Daiber et al., *Predigern und Hörern*.

31. Lorensen, *Preaching as a Carnivalesque Dialogue*.

message about the realm of God more precisely! While seeking to take account of listener perspectives, those empirical surveys still presuppose the transfer model as the implicit communication theory—albeit in a more subtle version.

An interesting exception is a Dutch survey from 1978 by the theologian Hans van der Geest who has a pastoral care approach to preaching. His empirical research took place in worship services held at a center for pastoral care, but he argues that his findings are relevant for an ordinary Sunday service as well. Van der Geest stresses the importance of the preacher's presence and personality in the pulpit and highlights the significance of the personal trust between the preacher and the listener. The preacher must have a personal relationship with God in order to be able to *preach* the Word of God.[32] I shall return to his research later.

Around the new millennium, there was a move in empirical research in Northern Europe normative/ideological approach to one that was more descriptive. Thus, the question of effectiveness was underplayed in the surveys and was replaced by a more phenomenological approach. Phenomenology is a disciplinary field in philosophy, not a research methodology like qualitative interviews and grounded theory. It is a direction in modern philosophy founded by Edmund Husserl who understands human beings as active co-creators of their own world.[33] A handy way to explain phenomenology is an "experience philosophy" aiming to investigate the way something appears in consciousness before being incorporated into a conceptual system. The phenomenological approach in empirical research can be defined as the study of structures of experience or consciousness. It is literally the study of "phenomena" as they appear in our consciousness, and the meanings we afterwards ascribe these phenomena in our experience. A researcher with a phenomenological study approach examines the data as it is experienced from the interviewees' point of view.[34]

The phenomenological perspective has been directional in the development of the empirical research methods. The starting point for phenomenology is neither idealistic or realistic; phenomenology seeks to describe the phenomena without considering whether they exist independently of

---

32. Van der Geest, *Du hast mich angesprochen* (translated into English as *Presence in the Pulpit*).

33. Phenomenology has been practiced for centuries, but it came into its own in the early twentieth century in the works of Husserl, Heidegger, Sartre, Merleau-Ponty et al.

34. Jacobsen et al., *Kvalitative metoder*, 186–88.

consciousness. The main theme in phenomenology is the intentionality of consciousness. The central structure of an experience is its intentionality, its being directed toward something, as it is an experience of or about some object. An experience is directed toward an object by virtue of its content or meaning (which represents the object) together with appropriate enabling conditions. The goal of a phenomenological analysis is to investigate the being of phenomena, and by describing distinct phenomena. Thus, researchers with a phenomenological approach, using qualitative research and grounded theory, seek to integrate distinct fragments in larger entities, and accordingly search for the phenomenological essences, discourses or conception.[35]

An example of the phenomenological approach is a Swedish survey aimed at describing the different concepts of preaching in play among preachers and congregation,[36] and a Finnish survey analyzed the different receptions of the same sermon, finding a need for the feeling of security.[37] Another Dutch survey, using both qualitative interviews and grounded theory, had a more dogmatic approach even though grounded theory is quite different from traditional research in that the researcher does not have an existing theoretical framework in advance. Due to the theological principle, that faith comes from listening, the researcher takes as the theological starting-point that the act of listening to sermons has a religious dimension. Consequently the researcher aims to investigate "what occurs religiously in the act of listening" and to account for this theoretically in terms of dimension, processes and types.[38]

Instead of assuming that the listening process has an inherent religious function, my starting-point was to investigate what happens when churchgoers interact with the sermon, and then set the results in relation to the theological conviction which ascribes a religious dimension to the listening process.[39] I wanted to investigate how listeners actually *listen to* and *interact with* sermons. Thus, I followed the more phenomenological approach to empirical surveys in the Nordic countries and was open to the possibility, without assuming it, that the listening process has a religious dimension.

35. Brinkman and Tanggaard, *Kvalitative metoder,* 46.
36. Almer, *Variationer av predikouppfattningar.*
37. Sundkvist, *En predikan.*
38. Pleizier, *Religious Involvement in Hearing Sermons.*
39. I made use of semi-structured qualitative interviews and constructing Grounded Theory. I will explain my methodology further in ch. 2.

My research question, therefore, was: "What happens when churchgoers listen to the sermon?" My focus was not on *what* the listeners had actually heard, but on *how* they listened to a specific sermon and interacted with it. When I began my research in 2011, there were no previous surveys in Denmark using empirical methodology in the field of homiletics, so I had to pave the road while driving. Subsequently, my results have inspired new research in the Nordic countries, which has been elaborating and expanding the idea of the Third Room of Preaching.[40]

Even though my point of departure was a descriptive approach, and the intention was to describe the listening process, the point of arrival was unintentional from the standpoint of more normative theological research. The empirical findings stress the importance of the preacher's person for the listeners' perception of the preaching event, which questions the Danish pastors' interpretation of the Protestant theological conviction on preaching that "through the word, as means bestowed, the Holy Spirit works faith where and when it pleases God."[41] Thus, the empirical findings and the theological convictions of the interviewed preachers were not consistent. This drew me towards the task of defining the implied systematic theological pre-assumptions in the preachers' convictions in order to see if it is possible for them to be consistent with the empirical experience of preaching.

As a result, the inductive empirical research journey brought me into a landscape of a more normative approach. If the dichotomy between human and divine agency had to be repealed, then it should be possible to articulate a communication theology of preaching where both the divine agency and the empirical experience—emphasizing that preaching is dependent on human agency—remain intact. I was investigating "The Word of God" as a less cognitive enterprise in favor of an understanding of preaching as an embodied interactive event situated in time and place in which the listeners and the preachers participate. In the search for overcoming the dichotomy, I entered into a more normative approach to the theology of preaching. I shall explain the content of the normative perspectives that emerged in chapter 2. After I had finished my research, I realized that I had been participating in an empirical movement in the Nordic countries using empirical methodology approaching normative theological research,

---

40. A research group in Norway has been working on an empirical research project with young people and children attending worship. Kaufman, *Mer enn ord*.

41. Especially formulated in the Evangelical-Lutheran confession, Confessio Augustana, § 5.

which is also an area of growing interest in practical theology in Northern Europe.[42]

These two approaches, empirical research and traditional theology, have generally remained distinctively different. The first belongs to sociological studies in religion and has pursued empirical knowledge to gain insight into life within the Church, but within a framework separate from the claims of faith. The second, traditional theology, working with the claims of faith, has an idealized approach to practical theology applied within the church, but distant from empirical research. However, as a new epistemological paradigm emerges in other disciplines, assuming that knowledge is always bound to the perceiving subject's participation in the cognition process, this epistemological development is also moving into theology. Consequently, the distinction between objective and subjective knowledge is breaking down and paving the way for empirical research into theology as well.[43] That is probably one of the reasons for the increasing interest in the practice of empirical theology. As previously described, there is a fast growing interest in developing and deepening the interaction between empirical research and theological reflection. A number of empirical research studies, drawing explicitly on the tools of empirical methods, have a theological openness which is new, and this development seems to follow international trends.[44]

Despite this movement in practical theology, empirical homiletics is still in its infancy. Empirical homiletics is an academic discipline of the future. I believe that we have reached an intersection of two different homiletic traditions, offered by two different perspectives and based on two different paradigms. It is not a matter of which perspective is right or which is wrong. It is more about the fact that different perspectives generate different kinds of perception, which will complement each other and maybe challenge each other in their dialogue.

Due to the traditional way of thinking of homiletics in Denmark, bookshelf after bookshelf of sermon collections can be found! The focus has been directed towards the theological content of the written words of the pastors' manuscripts; it is the homiletic results, rather than the process that

---

42. Scharen, *Explorations in Ecclesiology and Ethnography*.

43. I shall expand the epistemological starting point for empirical research in theology in ch. 2.

44. See Wigg-Stevenson, "Reflexive Theology" and "From Proclamation to Conversation"; Kaufman, "Normativity as Pitfall or Ally?" and "From the Outside"; Gaarden, "How Do We get out of 'the Paradigmatic Box'?"

occurs during the moment of preaching which has attracted attention.[45] There is plenty of theological inspiration for the preacher in the Danish theological tradition, especially with regard to the notion of the sermon as a Word of God.[46] In addition, Danish homiletics has traditionally been inspired and influenced by German theology. This Word-of-God perspective has become very important in the Danish context, not least due to a strong influence from dialectical theology throughout the twentieth century. This involves an ideology of the Word, which is thought to work independently of any human intervention—and sometimes in spite of it.

In the last two decades, however, North American homiletics has had a significant influence on the homiletic development in the Nordic countries. The inspiration has especially come from the movement, the New Homiletic, and to some degree from Other-wise Preaching. The essential shift of paradigm effected by the New Homiletic considers the sermon as an interactive event, in which the listener generates meaning in a dynamic interplay between preacher and listener. This has resonated in the Northern European context, where homileticians such as David Buttrick have been inspirational, especially in his description of moves and structure and his proposal to visualize rather than verbalize the theological points of the sermon.[47] Fred Craddack's inductive communication strategy has also inspired the Nordic countries with the use of anecdotes and storytelling in preaching.[48]

In *Other-wise Preaching* John McClure highlights the alienation and asymmetry between preacher and audience, and his call for *collaborative preaching* has in various forms been repositioned into a Danish context.[49] Danish pastors have found that participants benefit from the collaborative preaching practice, as the conversation in the group opens up both the

---

45. In contrast to English-speaking countries, Danish and the other Nordic languages have only a very limited number of readers, due to the limited language segment. This could be a very practical reason for the relatively small amount of homiletic literature. Sermon collections can be read by ordinary people, whereas homiletic literature primarily appeals to preachers, and there is no tradition of lay preachers in the Danish folk churches.

46. From Søren Kierkegaard and N. F. S. Grundtvig, to name two of the Danish theological sources known outside the country.

47. See, for example, German homiletician Nicol, *Einander Ins Bild Setzen*; Danish homiletician Nielsen, *Genopførelser*; Thøisen, *Dialog undervejs*; Andersen, *Teksten og tiden*; Asmussen, *Ord virker*; Swedish homiletician Sundberg, *Här är rymlig plats*.

48. Andersen, *Ordet der høres*.

49. Lorensen, *Dialogical Preaching*.

text and the participants.⁵⁰ Thus, there is a widespread understanding of preaching not only from the perspective of the Word-of-God theology as a one-way communication, but also from a perspective of the preachers' understanding of the sermon as an interactive event. How listeners interact with the sermon and create understanding is a new research area demanding further investigation.⁵¹ Clearly, the qualitative interviews investigating the way the interviewee experiences and perceives the world is a valuable method to gain insight into the preaching event.

1.4 DESCRIPTION OF EMPIRICAL STUDIES IN NORTH AMERICAN HOMILETICS

In the rejection of a homiletic aiming to transfer static biblical truths to passive listeners, the New Homiletic and Other-Wise Preaching draw on insights from a listener-centered rhetoric and assign human experience a crucial role. The listeners are creative agents and co-authors in the preaching event, relating what they hear to their own experience. Representatives of the New Homiletic have been criticized for their more general essentialist view of the listener. The preacher cannot appeal to a common horizon of experiences and thereby lead the audience to a particular "eureka" in the sermon, as Craddock suggested, since people do not *share* the same experiences. Thus, shared experiences cannot be a valid homiletic precondition for preaching. This view of human diversity, otherness, or strangeness is the basis for the new orientation in homiletic development, moving a step farther than the New Homiletic, is called Other-wise Preaching, and is increasingly characteristic of early twenty-first-century scholarship in preaching in North America. As emphasized by Other-wise preaching, there will always be an alienation and asymmetry between the preacher and the listeners—and among the different listeners. The homiletic core question is then how to preach in accordance with experience, when people do not share the same experiences.

The question has been answered theoretically, but why not take an empirical approach? The emphasis upon experience fits well with the perspective of empirical studies, which investigate reality the way humans

---

50. Christensen, "Collaborative Preaching."
51. It is very likely that such investigation is currently taking place in Christian churches around the world. For example, while writing this book, I came across another empirical research project in progress conducted in South Korea: Park and Wepener, "Empirical Research on the Experience."

experience it. A first genuine step toward empirical research can indirectly be seen in David Buttrick's homiletic from 1987. His internationally known book *Homiletic Moves and Structures* was based upon interviews with laity. Unfortunately there was no methodological awareness in this valuable contribution to the New Homiletic: no transparency in the empirical work; no explanation of the choices of methodology, no report of the working process, no available interview data, no self-critical reflection, etc.[52] Other empirical projects have been conducted in North America, most of them without any great impact.[53] Even the Academy of Homiletics has no permanent working group to sustain the academic conversation about empirical study in the preaching event—the research results, possibilities, and limitations of the different methods.[54]

An exception is the major empirical study of sermon listeners the Listening to Listeners project with 263 interviews of listeners in 28 congregations. The project involved one of the largest numbers of scholars and interviewees in a single research project. The results were published in four books and many articles.[55] The purpose was to identify qualities in preach-

---

52. Buttrick, *Homiletic*. Buttrick's empirical studies were based on interviews with congregations asking them what they remember immediately after having heard a sermon. The data was analyzed and interpreted through rhetorical lenses and provided the basis for Buttrick's comprehensive homiletic approach to structuring sermons.

53. For instance, Carrell, *Great American Church Survey*, conducted by Lori J. Carrell, professor of communication at the University of Wisconsin-Oshkosh, US. Her focus was on effective communication in preaching, and her intention was to compare and contrast the preacher's and the listeners' perceptions of the sermon. She found that listeners and preachers are partners in an interaction, and mutually responsible for the co-creation of meaning during the sermon. She concludes that sermons are not as effective or as dialogical as they could be, and in continuation of this she gives practical hands-on advices for how-to-do before, during, and after the sermon. Another empirical research project is carried out by McKinney, *View from the Pew*, which like David Buttrick's project does not operate with an explicitly formulated methodology. This is also the case for Bellinger, *Connecting Pulpit and Pew*. The author gives concrete suggestion for how to connect pulpit and pew, which is the aim of the book.

54. The Academy of Homiletics, founded in 1965, is a North American organization for teachers and doctoral graduate students of homiletics, primarily from the United States but also with members from the rest of the world. The Academy of Homiletics would profit from a working-group on empirical research into the preaching event, and the same can be said of the international organization Societas Homiletica.

55. The project is described in McClure et al., *Listening to Listeners*. Three more books present results from different perspectives, Allen, *Hearing the Sermon*; Mulligan et al., *Believing in Preaching*; Mulligan and Allen, *Make the Word Come Alive*. The study has generated several articles listed in Allen's paper for The Academy of Homiletics Annual

ing that help listeners to engage in the sermon or identify what prevented them *from* engaging.

The research design was formulated in advance and the analyzed categories were defined from the classical Aristotelian rhetorical tradition, the three means of persuasion: logos, ethos, and pathos. The interviewees were interviewed based on their general understanding of preaching and not on a concrete sermon they just had heard. One of the interesting findings was that sermon listeners hear more and hear better, when they believe they can relate to their preacher in meaningful ways.[56] This empirical research project has made important steps in the direction of understanding the listening process and not least in moving the discourse in the empirical direction and thus contributing to a new perspective in homiletics.

This impressive pioneering project had some built-in teething troubles within the research design. By formulating a research design in advance, the researcher typically used predetermined theories with their embedded pre-assumptions. One of the problems with sticking to already formulated theory or a specific theological understanding that the system can understand and accept, is that research results easily ended up in a predictable way. The research data was thus perceived through predictable glasses and the results accorded with the familiar paradigm. One of the big challenges in working with empirical theology is that theology already has an integrated worldview which accepts things we take for granted and never question. This is also the case with the Listening to Listeners: the project used rhetorical theory with a specific understanding of the very notion of communication. For academic theologians it is so easy to focus unilaterally on communication as a cognitive act aimed at persuasion, rather than mere human interaction not necessarily aimed at cognitive understanding. In chapter 3 I will return to the question of how we are to understand communication. Moreover, if the interviews had focused on a specific sermon and not on preaching in general, the researchers could have gained an insight into how the listeners actually listen to a particular sermon, rather than into the interviewees' own interpretation of their listening.

A stronger research design would have seen a more inductive research approach, or more precisely an abductive rather than a deductive approach.

---

meeting in 2007, "Listening to Listeners." Furthermore, a number of PhD dissertations in the field of homiletics have used the data generated in the study and others have been inspired to generate their own data. See McClure, *Preaching Words,* 75–76.

56. McClure, "Thinking Otherwise—A Blog."

Abductive reasoning is a form of logical inference going from observation to theory. Unlike the premises in deductive reasoning, abductive reasoning does not presuppose, or even guarantee, a conclusion. Abduction will be explained more fully in chapter 2. This would have included an open semi-structured interview approach allowing for a greater degree of unpredictability, as the interviewer has to follow the interviewees thinking about preaching rather than vice versa. Unexpected perspectives could thereby better have forced the researcher out of the paradigmatic box with its unconscious pre-assumptions. It is both difficult and crucial to go beyond our own preconceptions in empirical study. One way to work more abductively is to renounce theories and analysis of ideas in advance and instead let the categories emerge during the coding and the analysis process of the raw data. This can result in *unexpected* categories. Exactly such an open abductive approach to empirical research is part of grounded theory, the methodology used in my empirical homiletic research.[57]

The inspiration for my research grew out of the listener-centered approach to preaching embedded in the New Homiletic and Other-wise Preaching with their embedded sub-assumptions about the listening process. These assumptions are typically based upon *theoretical* understanding of a particular biblical text or theological doctrine that is articulated theologically and then applied to interpreting the listener's experience. The traffic travels one way on the bridge of interpretation: The theory and theology is used to explain what happens when people listen. However, the researcher seldom attends to what actually happens in the act of listening from the perspective of the listener.

Indeed, for a generation Fred Craddock spoke about sermons being "open-ended" in order to *allow* the listener to draw out the meaning of the sermon.[58] His inductive communication strategy presupposes that the preacher has the power to give listeners permission to create their own meaning, but the preacher is not in *possession* of such power that can assign the listeners their freedom—they have that freedom in advance. Even though many listeners may be socialized into thinking that they should get the transfer from the minister, they are still creating their own meaning. The right to interpret in accordance with one's own perception cannot

---

57. Allen himself points to this weakness: "In retrospect we should have begun with what people wanted to tell us about preaching as guides for developing our questions and theories," Allen, "Listening to Listeners," 69–84.

58. Craddock, *As One Without Authority*.

be given or taken from anyone. My thesis was that Craddock and many of his theoretical colleagues were nevertheless presupposing the transfer-model—just in a more subtle way.

Several attempts have been made to deconstruct the transfer-model, but in practice it continues to be quite resistant—popping up everywhere in contemporary homiletics—probably because of the lack of an alternative communication model or a communication theology to explain fully the preaching event. This book therefore aims to bring the homiletic discourse into a new space by presenting the concept of the Third Room which was inductively developed by listening to the voices of the listeners. My experience is that the notion of the Third Room will challenge some of the most taken-for-granted communication axioms in homiletics. I hope that the notion of Third Room can be helpful in the search for an adequate understanding of the communication theology of preaching. Yet, before presenting the Third Room of Preaching, I will give a study report in chapter 2.

2

A Study Report

THIS CHAPTER GIVES AN introduction to qualitative research and Grounded Theory, including the epistemological starting point of this study in relation to the new homiletic paradigm presented in this book. I shall account for the initial design, how it developed during the research process, and how the assumed paradigm was transformed during the progress of the work. With the intention of being as transparent as possible, I shall explain how data was analyzed and how the theory of the Third Room abductively emerged during the process of data analysis. Finally, I shall give a critical evaluation of the methodology, and point to what could be done differently to improve results.

2.1. AN INTRODUCTION TO QUALITATIVE RESEARCH

St. Paul's words in Romans 10:17 state (literally translated from Greek): "Then faith [comes] from hearing, and hearing through [the] word of Christ"[1] (au. tr.). In the Greek text, the verb "come" is not explicit, but it has nevertheless been understood as "comes" in the third person singular, and

---

1 The Greek text is: "ἄρα ἡ πίστις ἐξ ἀκοῆς, ἡ δὲ ἀκοὴ διὰ ῥήματος Χριστοῦ" in Nestle-Aland 26th edition. The question is, "Who or what initiates this faith to come?" The sentence "faith comes from hearing" is an indirect passive construction which masks the primary agency of faith. This verbal form implies that God is behind the mask, as only God can inspire faith. However, the passive construction of the sentence is open to interpretation. Gaarden and Ringgaard Lorensen, "Listeners as Authors in Preaching," 1. In the NKJV, this expression is translated: "So then faith cometh by hearing, and hearing by the Word of God." In the NRSV: "So faith comes from what is heard, and what is heard comes through the word of Christ."

A Study Report

hence, has been translated: "So then faith comes by hearing, and hearing by the word of God"[2] (NRSV). Regardless of the translation there is no doubt that the emphasis is on *hearing*—not speaking. That is one reason traditional Protestant theology of preaching ascribes an inherent religious function to the listening process.[3] Obviously it is too reductionist to state that faith comes from listening alone, for faith is a dynamic interplay of many factors—e.g., experiences and how they are interpreted, relationships, culture, contexts, and of course the confession of faith, but undoubtedly *hearing* the gospel is a prerequisite for the Christian faith. When faith comes from listening, it makes sense to listen to those who listen to sermons. Since there is an entire scientific discipline available in order to listen and learn, it is logical to use the qualitative research interview for a closer investigation of the sermon-listening process and the practice of Christian faith. As explained in chapter 1, this research methodology is a well-developed practice and has been used for decades in the social sciences, and it is now penetrating into practical theology as well.

"If you want to know how people understand, experience and interpret their lives and their world, why not listen to them?" asks Steiner Kvale rhetorically.[4] Kvale (1938–2008), a Norwegian professor of educational psychology, leader of the Center for Qualitative Research at the Department of Psychology at Aarhus University in Denmark, is a recognized authority in the field. He was a pioneer of the qualitative research interview in the Nordic countries. In the following description of the qualitative interview and in the empirical research presented in this book I shall primarily follow the methodology he describes.[5]

The qualitative research interview seeks to describe the interviewees' experiences of the world around them and the meaning they ascribe to the central themes in their lives. The main task in interviewing is to gain insight into the interviewees' perspectives, into how they perceive and understand what they experience. Interviews are particularly useful for getting the story,

---

2. Kvale and Brinkmann, *InterViews*.

3. The Augsburg Confession (the Confessions of the Lutheran Church) article V: "That we may obtain this faith, the Ministry of Teaching the gospel and administering the Sacraments was instituted. For through the Word and Sacraments, as through instruments, the Holy Ghost is given, who works faith; where and when it pleases God, in them that hear the gospel, to wit, that God, not for our own merits, but for Christ's sake, justifies those who believe that they are received into grace for Christ's sake" (my italics).

4. Kvale and Brinkmann, *InterViews*.

5. Kvale and Brinkmann, *InterViews. En introduktion*.

or the interpretation of the story, behind an interviewee's experiences—in this case studying the experience of sermon-listening and personal faith. The interviewer can pursue in-depth information around the topic under study, which is what happens while listening to a sermon during worship.

The qualitative method focuses on the ambiguous empirical world based on the utterances of the subjects being studied—their faith, understanding, and interpretation of the world. So far, there is consensus about the qualitative research method, but how the methodology and practice exactly are to be understood is not precisely defined. The fact that there is no single universally accepted definition is stressed by the different schools of qualitative research.[6] Each particular approach seems to depend on the discipline in which the methodology is used. Two different perspectives can be distinguished: a cognition tradition, or as part of the research process.[7] Cognition tradition emphasizes epistemological arguments and philosophical paradigms, while qualitative research as a natural part of the research process is not defined as a specific way of *working*. As argued in chapter 1, theological discourse is bound to human cognition, as it is impossible to leave behind our own subjectivity. It is therefore very important in homiletics and within practical theology to be aware of the epistemological paradigms. Accordingly, I operate with the notion of qualitative research in accordance with the perspective of the *cognition tradition*, and I have chosen the following broad definition, generally accepted in the research tradition:

> Qualitative research is multi-method in focus, involving an interpretative, naturalistic approach to its subject matter. This means that qualitative researchers study things in their natural settings, attempting to make sense of, or interpret, phenomena in terms of the meanings people bring to them.[8]

I have chosen this interpretive approach, since it fits well as a starting point for my research project. This approach aims to describe the listeners' experience of the sermon, without questioning whether there is a right or

---

6. The qualitative research interview presented and used in this study follows the methodology described by Mason, *Qualitative Research*, 2; Swinton and Mowat, *Practical Theology and Qualitative Research*, 29.

7. This involves a philosophical discussion of how the world is to be defined: as a social construction or as a "real" thing. Brinkman and Tanggaard, *Kvalitative Metoder*, 17–19; Mason, *Qualitative Research*, 2; Swinton and Mowat, *Practical Theology and Qualitative Research*, 29.

8. Denzin and Lincoln, *Collecting and Interpreting*, 3.

wrong way to listen. Kvale's point of departure is that the human being is an interpretive creature who actively co-creates their understanding of the world, which of course also applies to the researcher. Therefore, the starting point for the qualitative research interview is that data is not just "out there" waiting to be discovered. The task is not to make the interviewees deliver pure, uninterpreted knowledge which researchers can collect without contaminating or coloring it with their own biases. Qualitative research is not a technique to generate response unaffected by the interviewer and the context, as the researcher is not just "digging up" pre-existing data within the interviewees. The researcher and the interviewees s *generate* data during the interview *interaction*, situated in time and place.[9]

One of the differences between homiletic literature based on empirical data and homiletic literature based on traditional written sources, such as biblical exegesis, philosophy of language, systematic theological works, or books by other important historical thinkers, is that the researcher in qualitative research actively participates in generating the sources, while the researcher in archive studies attempts not to do so. It would be easy to think that empirical sources are more colored and influenced by the researcher who participates in the generation of data than one working with written sources. Nevertheless, experience shows the opposite.[10] One of the reasons is that the sources are *alive* and can contradict the interviewer; and, furthermore, they can pull the interview in a direction the interviewer did not expect. So, the sources can be quite difficult to control. It is much easier for researchers in archive studies to stay in their comfort zones at their desks defining, selecting, and delimiting the sources written in books. The meeting with the "real world" on the other hand can be irregular and unpredictable. My own experience was that the i intervieweess in my research sometimes took the lead in the interview and drew the discourse in an unexpected direction. The results of empirical research often actually *challenge* hypotheses, theoretical assumptions, and preconceptions, which encourages the researcher to a more nuanced or revised understanding—or even forces the researcher out of the paradigmatic box, as was the case in my study.

The interview is a place for the production of knowledge. Data is generated in a situational interaction between the informant and the interviewer in an interactive event. The place for this event, the context in

---

9. Kvale and Brinkmann, *InterViews. En introduktion*, 158.
10. Flyvbjerg, *Kvalitative Metoder*, 481.

which data is generated, naturally influences the gained knowledge. It matters whether the interview is carried out, for instance, in a church, or in a room related to the church, or in the interviewees's or the researcher's private home. The actual interaction between the participants also influences the generated knowledge. There is a mutual inter-dependence between the personal interaction and the production of knowledge, for the personalities obviously influence the generated data. These include the interviewer's way of listening, being present or absent, being empathetic, being receptive or assertive, all or any of which will influence the interviewees' responses. It is not possible for the interviewer to remove him- or herself from the research project, but as previously stated, this is not considered as "pollution" of data. It is simply the condition for all qualitative research that the data produced is not purified and without bias.[11]

Thus, the researcher is always personally involved in the research process, not as a distant objective observer or witness to reality, but as an active participant in the reality explored and as co-creator of the interpretation process. Accordingly, the goal of qualitative research is not to generate "clean and objective data" in order to gain knowledge about an objective reality. The goal is the greatest possible transparency in the process of generating and analyzing data about the reality to be interpreted by the researcher. Therefore, the intention throughout a research process ought to be transparency. This is achieved by explaining the researcher's methodology: how the interviews were carried out; the practical choice and challenges in relation to the interviews; clarifying the context, the time and place, and by representing the interaction in the interview; accounting for the strategy of the transcription; and providing an explanation of the analysis strategy and the choice of theory—or in other words being as transparent as possible.[12] This perspective requires that researchers have a high degree of self-reflectivity, are aware of and explain their own presumptions, write about their reflections, and thus enable the reader to follow the *process* of the research and gain a *contextual impression* of the empirical data. Otherwise, it is not valid data according to the methodology of qualitative research. It is therefore crucial to account for how data is generated—as I shall do when presenting my research design.

While data about an experienced phenomenon (e.g., how a specific sermon is experienced) is generated during the interaction of the interview,

---

11. Kvale and Brinkmann, *InterViews. En introduktion*, 27, 47.
12. Kvale and Brinkmann, *InterViews. En introduktion*, 253.

it is important to keep in mind that talking about the phenomena can alter or even transform the experience. Something happens the moment the interviewees talk about the experience, as a new awareness can arise and the experience can move from an immediate non-reflective impression to becoming a conscious and reflective experience.[13] This process of growing awareness, in which a change from an immediate to a reflective experience, can take place, happens by means of language. The language in question, however, is not understood as a tool to express elaborated and completed thoughts, but rather, it is a medium for the process of thinking. The expression of "pure experience" does not exist. It will always be an *interpretation* of the experienced phenomenon that the interviewee expresses. This is the premise for the qualitative research interview.[14]

This distinction between an immediate experience and a reflective experience can also be found in the Danish theologian Svend Bjerg's homiletic.[15] According to Bjerg, the concept of experience is a complex matter. He defines experience as a trinomial: 1) moving from an impression which is an un-reflected experience and thereby passive; 2) then the impression is communicated and becomes an active experience; 3) and finally the first immediate impression is transformed into a reflected experience. During this movement from immediate impression to reflected experience, a pre-linguistic reality enters into consciousness, so that language builds a bridge between experience and reality. The expression of the immediate experience paves the way for the reflected experience, and the reflected experience is the result of a sensuous and bodily experience, taking place within time and place.[16] Bjerg's trinomial definition of experiences explains well what happens during the qualitative interview in general, and especially in the research project presented in this book, as the interviews touch upon issues of faith and personal relations to God. For many interviewees, these tended to be an immediate experience transformed *during* the interview to a more reflected experience. A few interviewees expressed discomfort at

---

13. In the Danish language, we have two words for experience: respectively, a direct, non-reflected experience (oplevelse), and a conscious and reflective experience (erfaring).

14. Kvale and Brinkmann, *InterViews. En introduktion*, 53.

15. Sven Bjerg (b. 1942) was an assistant professor of systematic theology at Copenhagen University, and his thinking evolved from narrative theology to experience theology. He can be considered as representative of the New Homiletic in Denmark, but is unknown to English-speaking homileticians, as he writes in Danish.

16. Bjerg, *Tro og Erfaring*, 37, 42.

this, as worship for them was a private, meditative, and non-reflective zone. Other responded that they had never thought about the topic raised in the interview or even talked with others about it.

This point leads to the ethical aspect of the qualitative interview as the researcher moves personal and private experiences (in this case personal faith) into reflection in the public sphere. On the one hand, it gives the possibility to generate perspective about which we can only give suggestions; on the other hand, it demands a high degree of caution and respect for the interviewees's integrity. A way to respect the integrity of the interviewees is to work with full anonymity, even though this may collide with the qualitative ideal of transparency and the desire to determine data in its context as far as possible. However, the interests of the interviewee's integrity can take precedence over the desire for transparency in the research, which is the case in this project. Thus, I have removed the names and places from this book.

Additionally, the qualitative interview has the potential to be an event in itself, drawing attention from the situation, about which the researcher wants to generate knowledge. Thus, the interview and the reflection about the sermon easily could improve into a pastoral care situation as the interviewees talked about their own personal faith in relation to the heard sermon, and the interviewees were emotionally touched. Thus, it was important to stay focused upon the experience of concrete worship and sermon. Yet another necessary ethical consideration is that relationship between interviewer and interviewee is an asymmetrical relationship, as the interviewee is open, exposing pages of her mind about faith or doubt, her experience and current life situation—while the interviewer remains closed. This methodology requires that these ethical and practical considerations become part of the presentation of the research. As mentioned above, my experience was that the interviewees sometime took control of the interview situation, asking me questions about what I aimed for or intended with my research.

Even though the researcher decides how explorative or controlled they want the interview to be in relation to the studied topic, the interview tends to live its own unpredictable life, because the interviewees reflects upon their own experiences, which the interviewer cannot predict. This gives rise to a high degree of uncertainty and requires the acceptance of lack of monitoring of the working process. Furthermore, it is difficult both to outline what is relevant information for research and simultaneously to

A STUDY REPORT

be present and attentive to the inforinterviewee in the interview situation. An interview is literally an inter-view: a view at what is in between. The researcher does not have an over-view, but a view into what happens in the very moment of the actual situation between the interviewees and the interviewer.[17] The demand that the interviewer be fully "present" during the entire interview implies that the analysis process must wait. Thus, it was my experience that it was not until the time-consuming process of data analysis that I realized which information was relevant for the research project.

2.2. AN INTRODUCTION TO GROUNDED THEORY[18]

Previous empirical research within sermon listening has elaborated and expanded our understanding of the listening process by using predetermined theory.[19] Yet, as explained in the previous chapter, one of the challenges in sticking to already formulated theory is that the research tends to stay within the familiar paradigm and perceive the investigated phenomena through predictable glasses. It is a challenge to allow for *un*predictable results, which do not accord with the familiar paradigm. Nevertheless, it was my intention to let the empirical data propel my research in order to allow for a new empirical-based perspective in homiletics. Thus, I did not have a *theoretical* point of departure: instead I used the methodology of Grounded Theory, involving the construction of theory through the analysis of empirical-based data. The purpose of generating theory in accordance with the principles of grounded theory is conceptualization, i.e. the naming of the overall structures and patterns in data. Thanks to a systematic coding process, Grounded Theory can create hypothetical connections between concepts and characteristics, which can lead to new theory. This can sound abstract, and for a more detailed explanation of the

---

17. Kvale and Brinkmann, *InterViews. En introduktion*, 54.

18. The methodology was initially formulated by Glaser and Strauss in *Discovery of Grounded Theory*. For a more detailed explanation of grounded theory, see Glaser, *Doing Grounded Theory*. For the development from a positivistic approach to a constructivist approach, see Strauss and Corbin, *Basics of Qualitative Research*. For the development of a constructive approach, see Charmaz, *Constructing Grounded Theory*. For a split in the methodology and how grounded theory has been influenced by varying schools of thought over the years, see Ralph et al., "Methodological Dynamism of Grounded Theory," 1–6.

19. An exception is the Dutch research utilizing grounded theory, but still maintaining the Protestant dogma of preaching as having an inherent religious function.

methodology, the reader can see the professional literature.[20] Here I shall briefly explain Grounded Theory in relation to my research.

Often, we assume that we know "what's going on," as we already have an experience with and an understanding of the phenomena we wish to investigate, in this case the preaching event. For example, many academically trained theologians straightforwardly assume that the core of the action in preaching is that the congregation must come to an adequate *understanding* of the gospel, and that the preacher can use words as an instrument to create this understanding. Built into this assumption are several cognitive premises, such as that the preacher has the power to control the listeners' *production* of meaning, and words themselves *contain* a meaning. But what if this is *not* the case? Grounded theory can provide a way by which we can get behind our own preconception. This requires a tolerance of the feeling of being out of control from the beginning of the research process, until the relevant topics are identified, categories are built up, and a new theory is formulated on the basis of the hypothesis.[21]

Our understanding and experience are seen from our perspective, but we may have blind angles and spots for other and different perspectives. Without letting our own preconceptions block the view of the others, the main question in Grounded Theory is "What's going on?" The method does not aim to tell "the truth," but to conceptualize what is going on by using empirical research. For this purpose, Grounded Theory offers a systematic methodology to collect, codify, and analyze the empirical data obtained from qualitative interviews in order to generate a suggestion for new theory. Thus, the goal is to formulate new theory (or hypotheses for new theory), based on conceptual ideas developed through the analysis of empirical data. In many ways, Grounded Theory method resembles what researchers do when retrospectively formulating new hypothesis to fit data. However, when applying the Grounded Theory method, the researcher does not formulate the hypotheses *in advance*. The hypotheses come as a *result* and constitute a theory that is *grounded in the data*—and not the other way around. The methodology operates almost in a reverse way from research in the positivist tradition.

A study using Grounded Theory has *no theoretical framework in advance*—which is exactly opposite the North American project *Listeners to the Listeners*, using Aristotle's three means of persuasion as formative

20. See ch. 1, n. 21.
21. Glaser, *Doing Grounded Theory*, 11.

categories for research. Instead, the study shaped by Grounded Theory begins with just a question: How do people hear the sermon? The project then builds on the collection of qualitative data—in my case 500 pages of transcription of the answers to that question. As the researcher reviews the data collected and distinguishes repeated ideas, concepts or elements become apparent, when tagged with codes. For example, in my survey all interviewees without exception talked about their impression of the preacher.

The method is useful for organizing and analyzing empirical data, because it allows space for the unpredictable and the unexpected and is a way to structure an empirically unstructured reality. The method aims to develop new theory grounded in data, reflecting patterns in the empirical material. Theory growing out of data are more likely to resemble reality than theory, which is formulated from concepts based on experience or speculation about how think things ought to be.[22] Word by word all data is coded in order to determine what the interviewees are actually talking about, so that concepts are extracted directly from the data. As more data is collected, and as data is re-reviewed, codes can be grouped into concepts and then into categories. Thus, I could distinguish three different kinds of dialogical interaction. These categories become the basis for new theory (in my case study, the Third Room of Preaching). Thus, Grounded Theory is quite different from a traditional empirical model of research, where the researcher chooses an existing theoretical framework and then collects data in order to show how the theory does or does not apply to the phenomena under study.

First, in Grounded Theory the generated data is coded into broad categories of key concepts via *open coding*—categorizing what the interviewees actually talked about, for instance, the preacher, the interviewees' personal life, the room where worship takes place or the music. Some statements can contain several topics in the same sentence and must therefore be coded into several categories. For example, one respondent said, "When the preacher was talking about Jesus predicting his own death, I thought of my wife, who died two years ago." In this sentence, the interviewee talks about both what he actually heard in the sermon, and his personal life. After the initial *open coding* process, data is analyzed more directly in order to understand the characteristics of the categories called *selective coding*. Thus, the categories in the open coding often contain subcategories. For

---

22. Strauss and Corbin, *Basics of Qualitative Research*, 12.

instance, the category "the preacher" in the open coding was divided into subcategories according to the interviewees' *perception* of the preacher—whether the listener had sympathy or antipathy with the preacher. These subcategories again can often be divided up into new subcategories. For example, the sub-categories were divided according to the criteria on which the listeners grounded their sympathy or antipathy for the preacher, such as consistency among personal faith and the words of the sermon, the ability to be present, an open attitude towards the congregation, and so on. This division and subdivision creates an overall structure similar to the roots of a tree, which makes the material more manageable. The coded data is then analyzed in order to determine connections and relations between the categories, the subcategories, and their characteristics. This process is called the *theoretical coding*. For example, what is the relation between the listeners' impression of the preacher's personal faith and the listeners' dialogical interaction with the sermon? As a result of these coding processes, new concepts may emerge to point towards a new theoretical understanding.[23]

When generating new theory, it is not a question of acquiring as much quantitative data as possible in order to be representative. It is a question of generating sufficient data in order to form *categories* and the characteristics associated with those categories. The researcher is not aiming for representation, rather for variation, as the scope of Grounded Theory is not a specific group, such as the Danish churchgoers' way of listening, but conceptualization leading to a working hypothesis. The premise of doing Grounded Theory is not that the researcher produces objective data to be quantified but generates inter-subjective data to be *qualified* by covering meaningful connections, interpreted, and conceptualized by the researcher. A key notion in Grounded Theory is "theoretical saturation" which can be simply defined as data satisfaction. It is when the researcher reaches a point where no new information is obtained from further data, and further sampling of data will not lead to much more information related to their research questions. The goal is hence to generate the required amount of data that can form the basis for the formation of categories, and to bring coherence to the conceptual ideas. Grounded Theory therefore requires a certain theoretical sensitivity to data. The working process of coding the data is *in itself* beneficial for the development of theoretical sensitivity. Obviously, the formation of categories reflects the researcher's interpretation of the data.[24]

---

23. Glaser, *Doing Grounded Theory*, 21–33.
24. Glaser, *Doing Grounded Theory*, 9.

A Study Report

The logic of the methodology is neither an inductive nor a deductive way of reasoning, but what is called the *abductive way of reasoning*. Inductive reasoning develops general principles from specific observations, and the conclusion is probable, based upon the evidence given. In contrast, deductive reasoning moves from one or more premises to a logically certain conclusion. Deductive reasoning thus links premises with conclusions, whereby the conclusion is a direct result of the facts presented. However, creative ideas emerge neither from deduction nor from induction but from *abduction*. A handy way to think of abduction is as inference to *the best* or *the most likely* explanation. You move from some observations (meaning cannot be transferred from one consciousness to another in sermons) to the best explanation of those observations (the understanding of the sermon is formed by an internal dialogical response to the external words of the sermon).

Using *ab*ductive reasoning the researcher sets up a proposal for a theoretical determination of a given phenomenon which leads to new proposals—in this case the study for understanding of the interaction within the preaching event. The given phenomena in my case were the empirical findings of my research into the listening event: This can be described as an internal dialogue in which the listeners interact with the words of the preacher, and create a surplus of meaning previously not present in either the preacher's intent or the listener's frame of reference. Abductive reasoning is a way of generating explanations of the phenomena that meet certain conditions. The conditions in my own study were that the semantic meaning of the sermon does not belong either to the preacher or to the listener. I therefore propose, by means of abductive reasoning, that the phenomena of the surplus of meaning is *emergent* in the shared situation. This idea of the emergent sermon led to a new proposal of the sermon event as the "third room of preaching" in which not only the two—the listener and the preacher participate there is also a *third* dimension. The abductive reasoning imbedded in the methodology opened up the possibility for me to penetrate into what happens in the sermon interaction and hence pave the way for a theory of a new communication theology that is more adequate to what empirically seems to happen in the interaction between pulpit and pew.

In accordance with the methodology of Grounded Theory, the result of the research—the development of new theory consisting of a set of plausible connections between concepts or groups of concepts—should not be treated as empirical findings. It is rather the researcher's suggestion for new conceptualizations.[25] Thus, the notion of the Third Room of Preaching is not a reporting of statistically significant certainties but rather an integrated set of conceptual hypotheses developed from the process of analyzing the empirical data. Validity in the positivistic traditional sense is not an issue in Grounded Theory, which instead should be judged by four criteria: *fit, relevance, workability,* and *modifiability*.[26]

Fit has to do with how closely the concept fits the perceptions of the studied phenomena. A good and valid result will give a cross-bordering recognition, and a response like: "Yes, this is exactly the way it is. I had a feeling along those lines for a long time, but I did not (or could not) name it, or I did not have the courage to go through it, before I was told." Presenting the results, I often have this kind of response from those who hear about this approach for the first time. *Relevance* deals with the real concern of participants and captures the attention, not only necessarily because of academic interest, but because it intuitively *is* relevant. *Workability* is whether the theory can work in practice, can be applied to the reality and, for example, can explain how a problem can be solved. A *modifiable* theory can be improved by adding new relevant data to the existing data. A theory generated by means of Grounded Theory is never just right or wrong, but it can be more or less fit, relevant, workabile and modifiabile.

Grounded Theory was a useful tool that forced me to see the preaching event in a new way. I was forced "out of the old paradigmatic box," so to say. The analysis of the empirical data offered a new way of thinking that supports a new system of ideas and contexts. Thus, the results motivated me to rethink the implicit assumptions interwoven within both my own pre-understanding and with the theology in much historical and contemporary homiletic thinking. However, I am well aware that structuring data by means of the coding process in accordance with the principles of grounded theory does have a limiting influence. The researcher makes an overview based on the degree of simplification of the studied phenomena; and yet this overview may be an important step for homiletic development and hopefully lead to new insights. Thus, it is my hope that the results of this empirical investigation can be a stepping-stone for further homiletic development in order to formulate an adequate communication theology and to contribute to the didactic of homiletical teaching.

25. Glaser, *Doing Grounded Theory*, 3.
26. Glaser, *Theoretical Sensitivity*, 4–6.

A Study Report

2.3 THE TRADITIONAL HOMILETIC PARADIGM

The motivation for the empirical research grew out of my teaching homiletics, primarily inspired by literature from the New Homiletic, from Other-wise Preaching, and from my own rhetorical training. I was rooted in an Aristotelian understanding of communication.[27] These theoretical foundations include normative aspects of the listening process which I taught. Accordingly, I took it for granted that the primary goal of preaching is to guide the listeners to an adequate understanding of the gospel, and that it is the preacher's task to provide this understanding of who God is, what Jesus offers and requires of us, according to the preaching texts of the day. During my research process, however, this (unconscious) assumption was completely disturbed, and I was forced to rethink and elaborate my preassumptions, which raises a whole new series of questions and possibilities.

The basic communication paradigm embedded in the sources of my homiletical inspiration was the rejection of the transfer model—implicitly assuming that the kerygma without a fingerprint could be extracted from the text and then transferred by the preacher as a pipeline into the consciousness of the listeners—typically associated with Karl Barth's dialectical theology. For decades the theology with this implicit understanding of communication has influenced the Danish preaching tradition, probably because the Danes lack an adequate alternative communication theology. In dialectical theology, the preacher, when preaching the Word of God, simply transfers the Word of God, which is fundamentally different from human words. [28] "In preaching God presents what God wills to present, and will present."[29] When the Word of God is said aloud, it is expected to possess meaning that the speaker does not control or have power over,

---

27. Aristotle (384–322 BC) was a Greek philosopher and scientist. He stated that the rhetorical goal is not—as claimed—to persuade. Rather it is to find the "convincing" arguments in every case. The word "persuade" (in Greek, "πειθω") is a central rhetorical *terminus technicus*, often just called "persuasion." According to Aristotle, the core is established by means of the three different kinds of persuasion—logos, ethos, and pathos. In the Aristotelian tradition, persuasion has been interpreted differently: people have come to think of persuasion in a narrow way to prompt the other adopt my point of view. In a broader sense, as suggested by the Danish professor emeritus Jørgen Fafner, it can be understood as encouragement to create meaning. The latter notion of persuasion was my starting point: I understood the creation of meaning as a cognitive enterprise.

28. Barth, *Homiletics*, 44–55.

29. Barth, *Homiletics*, 49.

and under no circumstances is subject to the preacher's own authority. The preacher gives credit to God and lets the Word be preached.[30]

Of course, Barth's theology was developed independently of the linguistic turn,[31] so he had no awareness of the breakthroughs in language philosophy in and after his time. Unfortunately, in the lack of awareness of developments in the philosophy of language, the blindness of the listener's agency in preaching slipped into the theological tradition influenced by dialectical thinking. The semantic meaning is mistakenly often regarded as embedded solely in the preacher's words, as if words have an isolated meaning in themselves, regardless of the context in which they are used. Of course, the listener is not automatically perceived as passive, but there is a lack of awareness of the activity of the listener, or in which ways the listener actively participates in the preaching event, and how this activity can be understood in relation to God.

For this reason I was inspired by the New Homiletic and Other-wise Preaching which theoretically reject the transfer model and replace it with an understanding of the sermon as an interactive event, generating meaning in the consciousness of the listener in the dynamic interplay between preacher and listener, and is thus not understood as a one-way communication.[32] This, then, was my theoretical starting point, but I was concerned about two things, practically and theoretically.

Practically, this transfer of communication paradigm is highly persistent and hard to overcome. Even though theoretically executed for decades in academia, this understanding of communication is still alive and going strong in practice. One of the reasons is that we as preachers experience preaching from the perspective of the pulpit with a silently listening congregation in front of us. They do not interrupt or argue with us when they do not agree or understand our words. Rarely, if ever, do they report on what they actually heard in the sermon—just a "Thank you for a good sermon, pastor" in the doorway of the church—and if so, even more

---

30. Barth, *Homiletics*, 148.

31. The linguistic turn is associated with a development in the philosophy of language in the early twentieth century, in which language no longer is perceived as a neutral medium to describe an objective reality.

32. Furthermore, it is fundamentally wrong to do so, as "All the words we know are human words. We could not experience nonhuman words and therefore should not try to work with the assumption that God spoke a divine language that was translated into a particular human language." Craddock, *As One Without Authority*, 90.

rarely will the preacher ask, "Why was it a good sermon for you?"[33] As there is seldom a direct response to the sermon, it is so easy to assume that is possible for the preacher to transfer their perspectives in the sermon to their listeners, as if meaning could be transferred from one consciousness to another.

Theoretically, it was my impression that many scholars and preachers in the New Homiletic tradition still operate with some of the old assumptions embedded in the transfer model. I was concerned, for example, with the pre-assumption in Fred Craddock's homiletic which assumes that by means of an inductive communication strategy the preacher can take the listeners through the same inductive journey that the preacher has been through, and thereby should be able to permit the listeners their *freedom* in order to judge for themselves.[34] Craddock's rejects the transfer model—not because it is empirically questionable, but because he believes it is unethical in failing to allow the listeners their freedom. This requires that the preacher *possess the power* to grant the listeners their freedom, and to govern their consciousness on the track to the same "Eureka," as the preacher has experienced.

Other examples include Eugene L. Lowry, who assumes that the preacher can lead the listener's consciousness through the so-called "Lowry loop," imitating a movie plot, or Thomas G. Long or David Buttrick, who assume that by use of images, narratives, or small anecdotes, the preacher can regulate how the listeners create meaning in dialogue with the sermon. Although calibrated to experience rather than to "information," the new homiletic literature still assumes some degree of ability to control the production of meaning. This latter assumption is what I questioned.

During the research process, I came across a theoretical expression for what can be named "the ownership of the sermon," that is indicating those who possesses the power to process the substantial creation of meaning.[35]

---

33. A known Danish minister describes how he once went to a sailor who had been shipwrecked on a winter's day. The sailor had been interviewed for a newspaper and had explained that while lying in the water and waiting for rescue, he had come to think of what the minister had said on Christmas Eve in the Church. Therefore, the minister asked which words—implying the words of his sermon—could possibly keep the sailor alive in the cold water. The sailor answered, "The Lord bless you and keep you." Bjerager, *Det ender godt,* 170–71.

34. Craddock, *As One Without Authority.*

35. I am indebted to my former colleague, Erling Andersen, at the Pastoral Institute in Denmark, for this apt expression.

Many of the New Homiletic scholars and preachers have an overly developed sense of the ownership of the sermon. When the homiletical literature assumes it is possible for the preacher to form the consciousness of the listeners, then the ownership tends to remain in the pulpit. As long as the theory purports to indicate how listeners are listening, then theory remains in the basic assumption that the ownership of the sermon belongs to the scholar-theologian or the person who preaches. This assumption is even reinforced by many listeners who think of themselves as socialized and theologized into thinking that they should get the transfer from the minister, regardless of the fact, they create their own meaning. It was certainly the case in my study. Many interviewees apologized that they had not listened properly and could therefore not account for the preacher's words. They felt guilty for not being able to listen "the right way."

Other-wise Preaching, moving a step further than The New Homiletic, rejected the pre-assumptions of the common place of identification by means of shared experiences. I approved of this and agreed with the idea of respecting the otherness and strangeness of the listeners. I think the concept of collaborative preaching which has grown out of Other-wise Preaching is beneficial both for the preacher and the congregation. After a roundtable preaching workshop, the participants will carry the text with them, and it helps the preacher to have his or her understanding of the text enriched by other and different perspectives.[36] Nevertheless, I doubt the validity of the assumption that by inviting the congregation into the sermon workshop, and by listening to the different experiences, and by incorporating these experiences into the sermon, the preacher can *avoid the hegemony of experiences*. Implicit in this reasoning is the whole idea that preachers can own the experience of the sermon itself, even if informed by congregants.[37]

These were my serious concerns about practice and theory when I began my empirical research process, but I was not yet conscious of my own pre-assumption that preaching primarily is engaged in a cognitive *understanding* and that communication in general aims for mutual

---

36. An empirical survey about collaborative preaching stresses these positive experiences for the congregation, see Christensen, "Collaborative Preaching."

37. To be fair, *Other-wise Preaching* does not explicitly state that the preacher can control the production of meaning, but it is implied when McClure assumes that it is possible to avoid the hegemony of experience by bringing the listeners' experiences into the sermon. I shall return to this question later in this chapter.

understanding. And I was not aware of the "ownership" of the sermon until finishing the research project, as I shall explain in the following chapter 3.

2.4 THE DEVELOPMENT OF THE RESEARCH DESIGN AND HOW THE PARADIGMATIC BOX CRASHED

The Interview Questions and Research Question

At the outset, I experienced the same teething troubles as have many empirical researchers since the beginning of the 1970s. My approach was to investigate what the listeners had heard in order to explore whether there was consistency between what they had actually heard and what the preacher intended to say, but I ran into trouble right away. The original idea was to explore what each churchgoer in a congregation had heard, experienced, and understood of a specific sermon in a given service of worship, what this experience meant to the listener, and then to explore the pastors' intentions with their words, their preaching experience, and their theological understanding of the same sermon. In addition, my plan was to compare these two types of understanding.

My initial point of departure was to be as exploratory as possible in order to reduce my own influence and to let the interviewees lead. I focused upon the topic—what the interviewee had heard in the sermon—while giving the interviewees room to define the content of the interview and provide the information that *they* thought was important—not what I thought was important. Consequently, the interview questions—not to be confused with the research question—were kept to a minimum and formulated as open ended as possible. In formulating the questions, I was inspired by Thomas Long's distinguish between *focus* and *function*: "What the sermon aims to say can be called its 'focus,' and what the sermon aims to do can be called its 'function.'"[38] In accordance with this distinction, I assumed that the sermon had both an informative dimension—what the words are saying, and a performative dimension—what the words are doing. Therefore, I formulated only two questions:

- *What did you hear in the sermon?*
  (Resonating the informative dimension.)
- *Did the sermon do something for you?*
  (Resonating the performative dimension.)

38. Long, *Witness of Preaching*, 86.

In the very first pilot project, I asked the interviewee, *"What did you hear in the sermon?"* She responded: "Well, I heard a preacher who wanted to show his academic skills." Her interpretation of the preacher's intention was the first issue she touched upon. What she had heard was *inseparable* from her experience of the *preacher's person*. During the interview, she referred to her life experiences and past good and bad involvements with the church, and how her own faith and doubt intertwine, with just small fragments of the interview focusing on the sermon. I simply asked her these two questions, which was enough to make her talk for about an hour while I was listening, nodding, sometimes repeating her words, other times asking an elaboration of her words. I concluded, that the interview questions were effective in order to generate data about the listeners' experience of the sermon, but the research question—what the listener had heard—was not adequate. The interview had revealed much more than just the listener actual reception of a specific sermon. I realized that the notion of "sermon reception" connotes the transfer model as if listening is only about receiving a message. I had gained insight into not only *what* the listener had heard, but rather into *how* she had listened to, and interacted with, the sermon and the entire service of worship. Thus, a better expression would be "sermon interaction."

The Point of Saturation

In the first pilot project the interviewee knew she was going to be interviewed, but would people not being prepared be willing to participate in the project and how many interviewees was needed? The next pilot project was in response to a service of worship broadcast on the radio. The purpose of this pilot project was primarily to get a sense of the point of saturation and whether people not being informed in advance were willing to give an interview. In addition, I wanted to examine whether the interviews with radio listeners who did not know the preacher supported the experience from the first pilot project: that the listeners interpret the preacher's intentions behind their words, as much they interpret the semantic meaning embedded in the actual words of the sermon. Likewise, I wondered whether I would gain insight into how the listeners interacted with the words of the sermon. After the broadcast the radio speaker told about the research project and gave the radio listeners the phone number they could call in order to give an interview. The experience was that people were more than willing to participate. Ninety persons called. Out of conversations with 25–30 persons, I saw some patterns began to crystallize in the way the listeners had heard the sermon.

These phone interviews confirmed and expanded the findings of the first pilot project: When asked what they have heard in the sermon, most of the radio listeners whom I interviewed commented spontaneously on the preacher's person, her tone of voice, her choice of words and they evaluated whether she was trustworthy, authentic and preaching honestly from her interior life. Furthermore, they responded by referring to their own thoughts inspired by fragments of the sermon. They told about their life experiences (and few about their religious experiences) their current life situations and past experiences with the church, and their faith or doubt, and it was sometimes hard to recognize whether their internal dialogue activated by the sermon was actually in response to the sermon actually preached or was their own construction. If I had focused only upon what the listeners had heard, I would have had as many answers as I had interviewees. So once again, the interesting research question was not *what* they have heard, but *how* they had listened.

Another interesting feature of these interviews were the differences between written and orally generated data. Because of the huge interest in participation in the project, it was not possible to interview all the listeners. Consequently, some were asked to answer two questions by email. Unlike the oral interviews the written answers were relatively specific. In a few sentences the listeners reported what they had heard and could remember of the sermon, again just fragments, but not to the same degree intertwining with their own thoughts. Thus, the written sources did not reflect a dialogical interaction with the sermon in the same way as the oral sources did. In the written material, I could investigate *what* the individual had heard while in the oral material I could investigate *how* the individual had listened.

Based upon the results of the two first pilot projects, I adjusted the entire project. In order to generate knowledge about the sermon interaction I changed the research question from *what* the listeners had heard to *how* the listener had heard the sermon. Still, I kept the original interview questions. Even though the distinction between an informative and a performative dimension of the sermon was too reductionist, these distinctions were effective in generating data about the sermon interaction. The idea of holding the answers of the listeners and the preachers together was also adjusted. The focus point was not so much if there were consistency between the content of what was heard and of what was said, but rather if there were consistency between how the listeners had interacted with the sermon, and how the ministers imagined the listening process.

I thought I was ready to take off for the "real" research project, and the goal was to get approximately thrity interviews from five different churches scattered throughout the country. However, the first attempt to generate data failed. It was a Sunday morning in a small village church with baptism and many accompanying kids and parents not familiar with the service of worship. The noise was loud and so the question of what worshipers had heard in the sermon was irrelevant—the children's voices and crying drowned out attempts to hear the sermon. This experience illustrated clearly the importance of the context in which the sermon is situated. When the sermon could not be heard, it was more obvious to ask about how the entire worship had been experienced. Therefore, I added another opening question, thus, the three interview questions were the following:

- *How did you experience the service of worship?*
- *What did you hear in the sermon?*
- *What did the sermon do for to you?*

The pre-assumptions were adjusted on the basis of the experiences from these first pilot projects, highlighting the communication process in preaching as *an embodied interactive event situated in time and place* at the expense of a (dialectical/Barthian) theological approach to preaching that glorifies the cognitive understanding of the semantic content of the sermon as the word of God. This theological understanding of preaching is co-responsible for many sermons in Denmark that are professorial, lecture-like, and immunized against listening.[39] The accent upon the preacher's person shows that preaching is a personal and relational driven event that prevails over the very theological content of the written sermon. If operating with the "Word of God" as *a semantic category* the empirical experience will challenge the theological understanding of preaching. This was the case in one of the pilot interviews. A radio listener complained about sermons in the service of worship, because she and her husband always ended up discussing the preacher's person after the worship: "But it's not about the preacher's person; it is the Word of God," she said. Her

---

39. Nielsen, *Genopførelser*, 155.

theological understanding of preaching as the Word of God crashed with her own personal empirical experience.

However, adjusting the research design caused the breakdown of the assumed paradigm, even though I was not aware of the consequences of leaving the concept of preaching as a cognitive enterprise, in favor of an understanding of preaching as an embodied interactive event, where "the Word of God" is less a semantic meaning, but more an interactive event in time and place in which the listeners and the preachers are participating. As a logical consequence, the core question is not who God is, but how we can experience God. These were my first reflections and struggles to adjust theological conviction with empirical findings. It was a slowly growing realization throughout the entire research process.

The basic meaning of the term paradigm is "A typical example or pattern of something. A paradigm is a world view underlying the theories and methodology of a particular scientific subject."[40] The world view underlying the prevalent Protestant understanding of preaching is that the listener interacts with the word of God in, through, and beyond the discourse of the preacher.[41] Perhaps the greatest barrier to a paradigm shift is the reality of paradigm paralysis, caused by the inability or the fear of seeing beyond the current models of thinking. Yet, I was not aware of how the initial correction in the research question based upon the pilot projects—the shift from *what* to *how*—would lead me into another direction and to an unexpected paradigm shift in my search for an adequate communication theology.

Ready to Take Off

In accordance with the purpose of qualitative research, my project did not intend to be representative, but was aiming for maximum variation. Therefore, I was striving for variation in geographic, demographic, social, cultural, and ecclesial characteristics among the selected congregations. Automatically, this resulted in theological diversity among the interviewed ministers. I selected five services of worship scattered across the country in the following churches:

1. A city church with a wealthy upper-class congregation that is not very steadfast, not very concerned about their faith or the community

---

40. Paradigm definition from *Oxford English Dictionary*.
41. Pleizier, *Religious Involvement*, 1.

of the church. They are particularly concerned about their personal financial resources.

2. A small countryside church with an active middle class congregation with an inclination toward a conservative evangelical theology.
3. A church in an open state prison with a congregation consisting of men mostly socially disadvantaged, and the majority had not been accustomed to attend church before they were inserted.[42]
4. A big city church in the heart of Copenhagen, the capital of Denmark with a well-educated, privileged and active congregation.
5. A church in a large provincial town with an active mixed congregation consisting of both conservative evangelical and liberal theological members. The worship in this church was radio transmitted, thus some of the interviewees were radio listeners from other parts of the country.

To avoid worshipers listening more attentively than usual, I did not want the congregation to be informed in advance of my interviews. In order to reduce my bias I neither wanted to select my interviewees myself; nor to "disturb" the worshipers for ethical reasons: Their worship experience should not be disturbed by my interest in generating homiletical data. Therefore, I was looking for a design where the interviewees themselves signed up if they wanted to participate in the project.

Thus, the research project took place as follows: Right after the sermon, the pastors announced from the pulpit that they were participating in this project, which they presented briefly. I was introduced as a colleague and researcher fellow present in the worship, and from the pulpit the pastors urged the congregation to give an interview. When the churchgoers finished the service, they were handed a piece of paper, a questionnaire with the three interview questions printed on one side. On the other side was a description of the project, and they could indicate whether they wanted to participate. Before the worshipers left the church, those who wanted to do so had answered the questions. The questionnaire served two purposes: Partly it was a gear to get interviewees—the unpredictable number of people

---

42. In an open prison in Denmark the detainees are allowed to live more like regular citizens, i.e., they can choose what they want to do, such as go to church, to the gym or to do something else. For a description from an American perspective of the Danish prison system, see for instance, Reiter et al., "Denmark Doesn't Treat Its Prisoners like Prisoners."

who were willing to give an interview—and partly it served to sustain the interviewee's memory in the very interview situation. These answers formed the basis of the interview, which lasted approximately one hour and took place either the same day or the day after. The interviews were carried out in a house owned by the church in order to reduce distractions from outside—interrupting people, and from inside—emotional connotations activated by being in the nave or in a private home.

Although I got many written responses from each service of worship, approximately only a third wanted to give an interview, but that was enough. I got three to six interviews from each worship, and from the radio transmitted worship I had eight additional interviews. Thus, I ended up having 29 interviews with worshipers and five interviews with ministers, all together 34 transcribed interviews—eqivalent to 500 pages of text.

In the beginning of the interview I presented the purpose, the practical and the ethical information about the interview which of course was anonymous. The interviewees were asked whether they wanted a copy of the transcription. I only had the three interview questions from the questionnaire, but for the purpose of background information, I also asked about age, education, current job, and in order to get a sense of their relation to the church in general, I asked initially, why they were in church that day. Thus, the worshipers were categorized by:

- Gender: 13 men and 14 women.
- Age: From 17 to 91 years, with an average age of 60 years.
- Education/job: four uneducated, five skilled workers, 13 with middle education, five academics, one high school student, one retired which education and previous occupation were not specified.
- Relation to church: 18 were raised with Christianity, 11 were not.

I estimated that I had achieved the preferred variation among the random selected interviewees.

Transcription and Coding

No one speaks with dots and dashes, therefore, a written text of an oral speech will always be an interpretation. If more than one person is speaking, the transcription is also be an interpretation of the interaction of the conversation, thus, the written text can never be a simple, factual reproduction of the oral situation. In addition, the translation into English will blur some of nuances of the Danish language, which is always a limiting premise for a translation.

However, with this in mind, I seek to describe the interaction of the interviews as closely as possible through a literal transcription of the interviews.[43] This literal transcript thus entails repetition of words and sentences, expressions and interjections like "um, ah, hmmm" and sentences with incomplete syntax. Pauses and outbreaks, such as "long pause," "deep sigh," "loud laughter," "weeping" or "crying" were written in parentheses, as well as changes in tone of voice, such as "said hesitantly" or "with raised voice." Physical activities were also written in parentheses, such as the inforintervieweemant "thumping the table." When the interviewees used significant non-verbal utterances and used expressive body, I tried to capture the expression by making a comment on that, like "You are waving your hand away from your head, when I ask you, 'What you have heard in the sermon?'" Typically, the interviewees then interpreted their body language and formulated their thoughts, like "Yes, I can't remember the sermon. I'm not good at sermons. Normally I don't understand them." A few times, it was impossible to transcribe the entire sentence because the interviewee's voice was too soft, too mumbling or just coughing, or a sound from outside—such as traffic noise or music—drowned out the voice. The lack of words is indicated by brackets […] in the text. Brackets are also used in this book when the quotation has too long a detour or too many repetitions. For reasons of anonymity, all names and places are replaced with "xxx."

The time-consuming job of transcribing the interviews helps to create a more systematic sense of data, distinguishing patterns and structures, and therefore it is step in the process of analyzing. The entire transcription was coded line by line, and words by word using a data analysis computer software program (NVivo).[44] The use of the program supported a more systematic organizing and analyzing of unstructured data. Coding data in the computer program serves in the first place the purpose of gaining an over view of all data—the 500 pages of transcription, the video records

---

43. To take notes and record the interviews, I used a smart pen, which is a digital pen with a microphone and a camera at the tip of the pen. For a description of the smart pen see https://www.livescribe.com/en-us/smartpen/.

44. NVivo is is designed for qualitative research working with very rich text-based and/or multimedia information, where deep levels of analysis on small or large volumes of data are required. For further information see http://www.qsrinternational.com/nvivo-product.

of the sermons themselves (only for my own use, as I have promised all interviewees anonymity), my field notes from the services of worship, the sermon manuscripts—and to identify different tendencies. For instance, from these pieces of data, certain tendencies emerged, such as that 22% of the transcription of the interviews with the listeners was coded under the preacher's person, even though I did not raise that issue. The software helped me to classify, sort and arrange data, to explore issues crisscrossing the large amount of data, and to identify various trends, such as classifying the criteria for listeners' perception of the preacher and examining relationships in the data. In other words, the analysis of the interviews developed along with the coding of data.

The following categories, listed by frequency, emerged during the first open coding of the interviews with worshipers:

1) the listeners' life and faith,

2) the preacher,

3) the entire service of worship,

4) the nave,

5) the folk [state] church,

6) the concrete interview.

All statements in data could be placed under one of these categories which were not defined in advance but grew out of the systematic coding words by words. These broad categories contained related subcategories. For instance, the category "entire service of worship" contained the following subcategories:

1) the sermon,

2) music,

3) other churchgoers,

4) the Eucharist,

5) Baptism,

6) prayer,

7) readings from the Bible,

8) the blessing.

These subcategories again were divided into new and more specialized subcategories, such as the subcategory of sermon contained ten new subcategories reflecting the listeners' specific statements about their sermon experience. As explained earlier, this coding process—similar to the image of the root of a tree—provided a kind of structure of the unstructured data for the process of analyzing. In addition, the software was beneficial for the sake of the written presentation, as all quotation about an issue were collated in one category or subcategory. Thus, the coding process became a part of the analysis.

Opening the Door to a New Understanding of Communication Theology

My presentation in this chapter makes the process of research design, transcription, and coding sound pretty easy and well organized. However, in line with the concept of Grounded Theory, I experienced the entire research process quite challenging, mostly because of the feeling of being out of control—both practically and theoretically. In practice, I did not know, how many interviewees I would get in each service of worship, or who would participate—if any, or maybe too many. I did not know when the interviewees had time to give the interview. Often, I did not know in which direction the interviews were going, as I was following the interviewees' thoughts allowing them to define the content of the interviews. Theoretically, it was a challenge not knowing where the research process would take me because I did not know which theoretical dialogue partners I was going to use in order to illuminate the result of the analysis. I did not know whether the entire empirical research would actually be beneficial for understanding preaching, nor how long it would take to organize the unstructured amount of data in order to let new insights emerge. And I had no idea of the consequences of implementing methods from social science embedded another epistemological paradigm than the traditional theological, but I relied on the empirical methods and had to pave the road while I was driving on it.

The greatest challenge was not to lose a sense of moving forward while I had the feeling of being out of control, but to see beyond the existing models of thinking within the theology and homiletical theory in which I was trained. Early in the coding process it became obvious to me, that some of the empirical findings clashed with the traditional understanding of preaching in a Danish ecclesial context. Due to the strong influence of dialectical theology, the preacher's person is considered to be separated from the preacher's function. At the opposite end of the scale is the North American homiletician Phillips Brooks,[45] who emphasizes the preacher's personality. Moreover, I found a tendency among the interviewed pastors to consider the importance of the preacher's ethos for the preaching event as empirical event but inconsistent with their theology.

This tension results in two preaching theologies existing side by side, both an operative homiletic associated with a practical experience, and an ideological homiletic related to a theological ideal, linked to an image of God as transcendent truth about which the preachers can talk independently of their own personalities. It looked like a dichotomy where the theological conviction and practical experience were out of step. Of course, the empirical emphasis on the preacher's person called for theory about the preacher's/speaker's ethos, but I was also searching for theory to grasp the results. Instead of rejecting the self-evident empirical finding or the generally accepted theological understanding—God alone communicates and inspires faith—I was searching for a third way to comprehend the results.

I was forced to break out of the paradigmatic box and examine the undercurrent of assumptions embedded in the common understanding of preaching. Theologically, I was taught at university that Christian theology has always recognized a distinction between the act and content of Christian faith—defined by the two Latin terms *fides qua creditur* (the faith by which it is believed) and *fides quae creditur* (the faith which is believed.)[46] Embedded in this distinction is a dichotomy between an anthropocentric and a theocentric world view, a distinction which was (unconsciously) soaking the interviews with the ministers. Was it possible to overcome this dichotomy by rethinking the common presuppositions, which is taken for granted in the traditional theological way of thinking? While I was wrestling with the argumentation for why I could implement empirical

---

45. "What, then, is preaching, of which we are to speak? It is not hard to find a definition. Preaching is the communication of truth by man to men. It has in it two essential elements, truth and personality. Neither of these can it spare, and still be preaching. The Truest truth, the most authoritative statements of God's will, communicated in any other way than through the personality of brother man to men is not preached truth." "The truth must come really through the person, not merely over his lips, not merely into his understanding and out through his pen. It must comeback through his character, his affections, his whole intellectual and moral being." Brooks, *Lectures on Preaching*, 5, 8.

46. McGrath, *Christian Theology*, 570.

methods from social science into practical theology, I came across an essay: "Epistemological reflections on the Connection between Ideas and Data in Empirical Research into Religion," by the Dutch theologian Chris A. M. Hermans who writes:

> Once this dichotomy has been introduced it can never be bridged. But the theological model of incarnation opposes such a gap. Human beings are themselves by virtue of "being from God." Incarnation refers to human participation in God, which is seen as a gift of divine grace. The antithesis of divine and human actions is false. In the act of faith, the initiative is reversed: God takes over, leading human beings into In/finite time and space, which is God. Finitude is not infinitude, but it is open to it. Hence we opt for a theological model of transcendence-in-immanence. There are traces and signs of a transcendent reality in our immanent reality.[47]

This paragraph opened the door for a new paradigmatic understanding of the preaching event. This could explain why the preacher's person was so important for the listener's sermon interaction. The dichotomy between human and divine agency is false. By following this track in which *incarnation refers to human participation in God*, it is possible to articulate a communication theology of preaching where the divine agency remains intact without neglecting the empirical experience that preaching is dependent on human agency. According to Dietrich Bonhoeffer, incarnation refers to a double movement in which God by entering the world, assimilates the world into himself.[48] In the incarnation God united himself with both humanity in general and the individual human. Thus, God is resident in each of us—not as a stranger, but as the very most personal.

What will applying this concept of God mean for preaching? How will the preachers' personal relationship with God—or participation in God—be reflected in their sermons? Following the idea that God takes over, leading human beings, including preachers, into In/finite time and space, which is God, the question emerges, "How can the preacher's personal spiritual life be separated be from the practice of preaching? And how are preachers to be trained homiletically?" Probably not by a lecturing professor telling the students what to say! The search for an adequate understanding to

---

47. Hermans, "Epistemological Reflections," 97. Chris A. M. Hermans is a professor in pastoral theology, Radboud, University Nijmegen, Nederlands.

48. This thought is part of the thinking of the German theologian Dietrich Bonhoeffer. See for instance, Bonhoeffer, *Min tid er I dine hænder*. Mikkelsen et al., *Liv og konsekvens*. Because of linguistic conventions, I use masculine pronoun for God.

bridge the empirical findings and the theological conviction raised a lot of new questions during the analyzing process and continues to press those questions.

Yet another interesting feature emerging during the process of coding and analyzing was that the creation of the *substantial meaning* of the sermon. The creativity of the listeners' interaction with the preacher's words was profound. The sermon they referred to often appeared as a different—and sometimes even totally divergent discourse compared to the one held by the preacher, so it seemed like a new sermon with a different semantic meaning. The substantial meaning did (of course) not belong to the preacher's manuscript on the pulpit. By investigating the ways the listeners create their meaning, the dialogical nature of the interaction of the sermon became evident. This finding sent me on the track searching for an adequate communication theory. Partly I found it in the Russian language philosopher, Mikhail Bakhtin and partly in Barnett Pearce.[49]

According to Bakhtin and Pearce, dialogue is crucial, not only to human communication but also to human processes of reasoning and understanding. Pearce provides understanding of how individuals create, coordinate and manage meanings in their process of communication. Bakhtin describes how reasoning is formed by a dialogical response. Interaction and the words of others provide the epistemological foundation for creative thinking and the development of individuals. I used Bakhtin's emphasis on dialogue as crucial to processes of understanding, to explain the interviewed churchgoers as the primary authors of the sermon. This authorship, evident in all the interviews, emerged from the listeners' interaction with the sermon which caused an internal dialogue. Rather the worshipers were to be seen as the primary authors of preaching with the preacher in the role of a co-author.

However, I improved this understanding after I have been working with the analysis in dialogue with John McClure's Other-wise preaching. He argues that the "idea of *proximity* requires that we get into the lives of people through a specific, local, and embodied interaction, rather than generalizing their experience towards either humanist or Biblicist rhetorical constructs of the hearer in preaching."[50] By the face to face encounter in collaborative

---

49. Mikhail M. Bakhtin (1895–1975) presented in Lorensen, *Preaching as a Carnivalesque Dialogue*. Barnett Pearce (1943–2011), see Pearce, *Kommunikation og skabelsen af sociale verdener*.

50. McClure, *Other-wise Preaching*, 49.

preaching it should be possible to avoid "hegemonic experience." But the empirical results did not sustain the idea of being able to "get into the lives of people through a specific, local, and embodied interaction." Rather the empirical data showed that there is "a blind spot" within the listeners, even for the listeners themselves. The experiences which the interviewees used to create meaning and understanding did not emerge until the very moment of worship in the liturgical setting, the singing, the prayers etc. I questioned whether the experiences would emerge in the same way in a collaborative preaching situation. Thus, this critical dialogue with Other-wise Preaching paved the way for the acknowledging of the "third agency" in preaching, emerging in the worship situation which lead me to theory of the Third Room of Preaching. In chapter 3 I shall explain how the theory has been elaborated theoretically subsequently, but before that, I shall critically evaluate the method by which I formed the theory.

2.5 CRITICAL EVALUATION OF THE METHODS OF RESEARCH

The premise of the qualitative interview involves considerable sensitivity towards the persons interviewed as well as self-awareness on the part of the interviewer and the preacher announcing the research opportunity from the pulpit. This process has some built in limitations. The recruitment of interviewees relies on the participating preacher's ethos and generous presentation of the project from the pulpit. If the congregation did not like their preacher they had probably not been willing to give an interview, so undoubtedly the preacher's ethos influenced the recruitment of interviewees, and consequently it can have reduced a more critical evaluation of the sermons—though this factor might be somewhat less in the case of the radio listeners who did not know the preacher.

The generation of data was also influenced by the interviewee's impression of me as the interviewer, and our mutual interaction within the interview situation. The fact that the worshipers were informed that I as the researcher was a pastor-colleague—and not for instance an organ player or social-anthropologist—probably influenced the interview situation too. Being familiar with the church could easily lead to identification with the church, which may have limited the interviewees' critical utterance about the church, the service of worship, the minister or it may even have paralyzed the willingness of potential interviewees to participate in the research. These are some of the limitations of the methods.

A Study Report

The advantage, however, is that the interviewees could ascribe credibility or authenticity to me as the interviewer, which may have facilitated confidence and trust in the interview situation, which is required for the interviewees to letting the interviewer have a window into their personal faith. In relation to interviewed pastors, it may have affected the interviews as well, knowing I was a colleague familiar with their working conditions and their implied theological language and terminology. While that sense of familiarity may have been beneficial to building up confidence in the interview situation, the downside may have been that I did not ask enough curious questions or follow up topics or issues, which an external interviewer may have done.

I had to be very careful that the interviews did not develop into pastoral care situations, a danger that resulted partly because the interviewees perceived me as a minister, and partly because the worship experience and the subsequent interview brought together personal life, faith, religious experience and current life situations. In addition to the practical and ethical information about the interview, the introductory information served the purpose of defining and clarifying the interviews as different from pastoral care situations. If the interviewees were to be emotionally affected during the interview, I did not intend to follow that track, but it turned out to be a delicate balance for me to gauge the border between an interview and a pastoral care situation. The interviews were carried out within an ethical gray area balancing between, on the one hand, respecting the interviewee's integrity and, on the other hand, following the research interest of moving personal experiences and faith into a public sphere of reflection.

It turned out in some of the interviews that the very moment the interviewees talked about their private worship and preaching experience, and the experience itself was subject of reflection, their perception of what had happened in the experience was transformed. According to the Danish homiletican Bjerg mentioned earlier in this chapter, the experience moved from an un-reflected area of impression, and during the interview was transformed to a reflected experience. A few of the interviewees found this process challenging because their personal faith and religious experience resided in their private sphere, and belonged to meditative zone "free of reflection," as one of the interviewees articulated it. So the method operates in an area where the interviewees are often not accustomed to expressing their experiences and reflecting on them. The benefits for a new area of research is obvious, but also the limitations—and one of them is my partial perspective. It would have been productive to have had more researchers with different perspectives to evaluate and analyze the generated data.

My approach to the empirical research is of course based on my theological and homiletic horizon of understanding as well as my professional and personal experiences. One of weakness was that I was not educated as a sociologist trained to use the empirical methods and had to gain knowledge and experience with the empirical method initially and during the research process. One of the positive factors was, however, that I know the subject to be studied very well from perspectives of the pulpit, the pew, and the homiletical teacher in the classroom. A sociologist, anthropologist or psychologist with different professional perspectives who also wanted to investigate the sermon interaction might have come to alternative results, but according the criteria prescribed by the methods, it does not mean that the results are wrong. The research would just have had different strengths and weaknesses, which usefully could have complemented each other. This is exactly the reason for writing this book—inviting other researchers with their different perspectives to participate in the interpretation of the generated and here presented and analyzed data. This is my hope.

3

Exploring the Third Room in Preaching

CHAPTER 3 SHOWS HOW the notion of the Third Room of Preaching developed during the analysis of the interviews with churchgoers and preachers, and explains how the theory has been elaborated theoretically subsequently. I shall present five main results of the analysis: 1) the significance of the preacher's ethos, 2) the reciprocal relationship between the preacher and the listener, 3) the different dialogical interactions with the sermon, 4) the importance of the listener's situated starting point, and 5) the sermon as an inter-subjective production of meaning. In each of these sections, I first present the empirical analysis and aim to describe the listeners' empirical experience of the sermon without being normative or judging whether it is a right or wrong, good or bad way to listen. Then, I discuss the results, and present adequate theory to illuminate the findings.

3.1 THE SIGNIFICANCE OF THE PREACHER'S ETHOS

> Well, ... I can tell you, if I don't have—what shall I say—sympathy for those who are preaching, the sermon can be just good, but it doesn't have any impact on me.[1]

At a surface level, the role of ethos in the listening experience is crucial. Even though it was not a part of the research design, all the listeners spontaneously talked about their experience of the preacher when they were asked to respond to the service and the sermon in general. Often the

---

1. 80-year-old retired man, member of the parish council for 40 years, in periods also chairperson of the congregation.

interviewees talked about their experience of the preacher's person right from the beginning. More than 20% of the interviews with the listeners addressed the preacher's person, which was also the case for the interviewees from the radio-casted worship even though they did not know the preacher in a personal way, they, too, talked about their impression of the preacher, according to tone of voice, content of the sermon, and their interpretation of the preacher's intension.

As background information, I wanted to know whether the interviewees were familiar with the church and were regular churchgoers. So to generate knowledge about their motivation to attend worship service, their pre-understanding of the gospel and Christianity, and their prerequisites to participating in the worship service, I asked initially: "Why were you in the church today?"[2] As expected the question resulted in answers providing information about the interviewees' relation to the church, but in addition, they also highlighted the significance the congregation ascribed to the pastor. For instance: "I was curious to hear xxx (name of the pastor) preach, since I've heard a lot about him." I was surprised as many of the interviewees related their presence in the church that day by explicitly pointing to the pastor: "I'm here today, because it is long time since I have heard NN preach." or "I didn't like the way the pastor buried my wife in my own church, therefore I worship here."

The listeners based their presence in the church on their relation to and their experience of the pastor: "I very much like our pastor here in our church;" and for some of the interviewees their presence was even determined by the pastor despite their faith: "I don't know whether I believe in God, but I believe in our pastor. She is great." It is remarkable that none of the interviewees based their presence in church on their relationship to God, when they were asked about why they attended worship that day, but in several ways pointed to the preacher.

Empirically it was evident that the basic question of the listener's sympathy or antipathy with the pastor is important for the preaching event. The churchgoers' experiences of the service, the sermon, and the preacher are intertwined in an inseparable way. The pastor's person and the pastor's function merge in the listeners' experience of the worship, and there was a tendency that the impression of the pastor's ethos is superior to the

---

2. In contrast to the many different denominations in North America where the question could explore the relationship to a specific denomination, the same question in the homogeneous folk church in Denmark would explore whether the interviewees had a relation to the church or not.

content of the actual sermon. For example, some interviewees said that they liked the pastor very much, even though they did not understand the sermon. Or they did not agree with the pastors' interpretation of the text, but appreciated the pastor—"He is a great fellow." So, the cognitive understanding is subordinate the experience of the ethos and the relation to the preacher. Sympathy—from the Greek word συμπάθεια, *syn* "together," and *pathos* "feeling"—is like a connector that plugs into a wall outlet. When the listeners have sympathy with the preacher, the emotional connector is plugged in, and they listen and process the words of the sermon, regardless of whether they agree with the preacher or not, and conversely, if they do not have sympathy, they do not listen. The listeners' utterances about their *sympathy* with the preacher emphasizes that the emotional and relational dimension of preaching as a *precondition for the cognitive dimension*, and that hearing a sermon is about more than just understanding a message.

The next step in the analysis was then to investigate what constitutes the experience of sym- or antipathy. Although I expected external factors like sex, age, color, race,[3] appearance, rank and authority established through ministry to be important factors, these were not topics discussed by the churchgoers. Rather, the most important factors were whether the listeners experienced the preachers as being themselves, engaged, and present, and whether the preachers stood behind their words, were faithful to their own faith and were preaching from their hearts. The interviewers frequently touched upon these issues. In addition, the listeners considered whether the preachers have a respectful, non-judgmental and open-minded attitude towards the congregation. So two main characteristics emerged as crucial criteria's for the constitution of the listeners' sympathy with the preacher and thereby willingness to listen to the sermon, namely *authenticity* and *attitude*. Thus, it is was not primarily—as I as an academic trained theologian could expect—the preacher's theological content of the sermon, and ability to conceptualize statements about God, but of the experience of the presence of God incarnated via the preacher and the entire service of worship.[4]

---

3. The question of color and race is not an issue in the Danish Church in the same way as in the multi-ethnic US because of the traditional homogeneous ethnic population in Denmark, but with the increasing immigration of Christians from other nationalities and converts it is a coming up issue.

4. This is a controversial finding in a church tradition strongly influenced by "The Word-of-God-theology."

The Third Room of Preaching

Authenticity

> I like listening to pastors who, I feel, believe what they are preaching.[5]

The listeners relate positively or negatively to the preacher, according to whether they perceive the preacher as authentic. Listeners consider preachers as authentic when the listeners experience preachers as being themselves, having integrity, being engaged and personally committed, and not least are true to their own faith: Not only is the churchgoers attention directed to the content of the sermon, but also to the preachers' personal relationship to their own words: "I experienced a preacher who wanted to show his academic skills."[6] The listeners interpret the preachers' intention with their words and whether it means something for the preachers themselves. The listeners sense whether the sermon on a personal level is vitally important for the preacher and whether preachers believe in what they are preaching.

Even though the listeners do not understand the content of the words, they understand whether the messages mean anything for the preachers themselves, whether they speak from the hearts, or whether the sermon are just theological acquired knowledge without any existential significance for the preachers themselves. "I stop listening when the sermon is just an enumeration of theological clichés. It is uninteresting." So the preacher's faith is crucial for the listeners and especially both *consistency between the preacher's words and preacher's faith*. Otherwise the sermon is experienced as dull and uninspiring for the listener.

Of course, the preacher's theologies and academic knowledge have an impact on the churchgoers, but theology and knowledge are subordinate to their desire for an authentic and attentive preacher with an open-minded attitude toward the congregation. It matters whether the churchgoers can identify themselves with the preacher's theological perspective and faith tradition, but the preacher's integrity is more essential. Otherwise the sermon becomes "irrelevant." For instance, an interviewee did not agree with a pastor's evangelical theology, it "was too dark. I missed the joy and the spark in his personal faith." Nevertheless, the listener perceived the preacher as authentic because "He believed in it himself." The listeners' interactions with the sermon are not necessarily dependent upon the preacher's

---

5. 60-year-old man who is regular churchgoer.
6. 54-year-old woman not familiar with the church.

theology—as the listeners do not take over the preacher's point of view. Listeners are more dependent on the preacher's ability and willingness to be true to the preacher's own faith. Authenticity and being faithful to own faith are thus key concept in the preaching event, which the churchgoers regardless of age, gender, religious and educational background, employment, or life circumstance appreciated. Both the 80-year-old man who was of member of the church council for 40 years—quoted in the beginning—and a 17-year-old female cantor, with no strong relationship to the church, appreciated preachers being authentic, speaking from the heart and being true to their own faith, even though they did not agree with the theologies.

The request for an authentic preacher could sound like an excessive and unfair claim to put on the shoulders of the preacher, who after all is just a human being with faith and doubt (the laity have not patented doubts). Clerics may perceive it is an unreasonable and an overloading of the office of the pulpit. Indeed, it is easy to understand the theological necessity to protect the ministry against unrealistic demands and unreasonable expectations from a secularized congregation. Many ministers are trained to think they should provide great faith trough a sermon with deep spirit and power to persuade the congregation to the right theological beliefs. If the quest for an authentic preacher is understood this way, it is of course an unfair and unrealistic demand, but I do not interpret the request for authenticity this way. It is not a question of possessing a certain degree of faith or piety, or being able to believe in a certain way. It is more a question of preachers being honest to own faith, which also implies being doubtful, uncertain, or hesitant, which are essential parts of authenticity.

Authenticity from the perspective of the pew is *not* constituted by either performance or achievement—but by *courage*:

- The courage not to perform,
- the courage to believe,
- the courage to be faithful to own faith and doubts,
- the courage just to be oneself with vulnerability, weakness, and uncertain spots,
- the courage not to pretend to be someone else,
- the courage to service and share the encounter with the gospel with the congregation.

Authenticity grows out of the consistency between the preacher's inner faith and their outer words. The churchgoers appreciated preachers who have the courage to be authentic because autenticity affected *their interaction with the sermon.*⁷

Attitude

> Our pastor, she is so nice, warm and open, you cannot help caring for her. She is so personal in what she is saying, and she also try to speak personally to you, so you cannot avoid listening to what she is saying.⁸

Also essential for the listeners' experience of the preacher's ethos is the preacher's *attitude* towards the congregation. An open minded, respectful and non-judgmental attitude supports listening, whether the listeners agree or disagree with the preacher's interpretation of the text. The attitude is interpreted via nonverbal expressions such as body language and gestures, eye contact, tone of voice:

> The pastor tried to smile and have eye contact and to be human behind his ecclesiastical dress.⁹

The attitude is also interpreted and through verbal expressions, and whether the preachers strive to communicate their theological knowledge in a clear an understandable way for the listeners:

---

7. While I was working on the empirical analysis of this book, a discussion took place in the Danish newspaper caused by a church council applying for a new pastor with "faith," which may sound odd to a North American. But there has been no theological tradition in Denmark for perceiving the preacher's personal faith as a relevant homiletical issue. The pastor's faith used to belong to the private sphere, and the argument was that "preachers should be judged by their preaching, not by their faith," understanding that personal faith and preaching can be distinguished, as well as person and communication. This implies an understanding of communication as transport of information from one person to another, the so-called transfer model inconsistent with empirical research. This insight stresses the need to formulate an adequate communication theology to replace the transfer model.

8. A 60-year-old man familiar with the church.

9. A 44-year-old woman not familiar with the church. Her comment about the pastor's dress refer to the long black dress with a white ringed ruff used in the Danish church by all pastors. The robe is the pastors' "uniform" or official dress. In the seventeenth century the king prescribed the use of the white ruff that pastors still use together with the black robe. The law of the church says that the pastor has to wear the robe at all church services and rites.

> Sometimes the preachers express themselves in such a complicated way you need to be a preacher yourself to understand. I like when it is said in a vernacular way, that everyone can understand.[10]

An open, welcoming, respectful and non-judgmental attitude from the preacher's side encouraged the listeners' willingness to interact with the sermon, whether the listeners agreed or disagreed with the sermon: the adjective "*open*" appeared many times in interviews in relation to the preachers' attitude as a positive determination. To be open is a precondition for being able to have contact, and both the listeners and the preachers talked about the importance of having contact with one and another. The quest for an open attitude again emphasizes the non-cognitive dimension of preaching and the importance of the reciprocal relationship between listener and preacher, which I shall account for in a following section, but next I will turn to the theoretical explanations and the theological implications.

The Empirical Findings of Ethos in Dialogue with Theoretical and Theological Considerations

The listeners' highlighting of the preacher's authenticity and open attitude makes the *person* and the *relation* crucial for the preaching situation. The importance of the personal and relational dimension of ministry is also found in other international imperial research into the sermon listening process.[11] For instance the Dutch pastor, Hans Van der Geest, wrote in 1978 that one of the most important aspects of preaching is the personal trust between the listener and the preacher.[12] The preacher's personality is crucial for the encounter between the listeners and God. In an ideal world, preachers see themselves as belonging to God, and in a personal way, they communicate this personal relationship with God to the congregation. This requires that preachers are in touch with themselves, acknowledge their uncertainty and the unenforceability of their messages, and, in addition, dare to disclose themselves and stand by their personal faith and doubt.[13]

---

10. A 69-year-old man, chairman of a church council.

11. The South African homiletican Malan Nel has come to a similar conclusion in his empirical research which unfortunately is not translated from Africaans, see *Ek is die verskil.*

12. Van der Geest, *Du hast mich angesprochen.* Van der Geest had a pastoral care approach to preaching. He supervised other clergy undertaking Clinical Pastoral Education in a Swiss hospital, and his empirical research was conducted there.

13. For Van der Geest, the innermost element of the human being is defined by the

Also the North American project from 2014, the Listening to Listeners project:[14] "discovered that sermon listeners hear more and hear better when they believe they can relate to their preacher in meaningful ways."[15] A Norwegian empirical research from 2014 conducted by pastor Hilde Fylling, argues that the interviewees were consistent in agreeing about what makes a good sermon: The preachers must be themselves, believe in what they are preaching, and the listeners have to experience the preacher as being present and engaged. What really matters for a good sermon is the pastor's commitment and authenticity.[16]

For some it may seem evident that person and relation are precondition for an interaction with the theological content of the sermon. But many theologians and ministers find it challenging to move beyond thinking that the sermon is entirely the Word of God independent of human beings and exclusively written in the Bible. However, from the perspective of the pew, the living voice of the gospel needs a preacher whom they perceive as human and authentic.

I searched for a communication theory to illuminate the personal and relational dimension of the preaching situation. From a classical rhetorical point of view, it is not surprising that the listeners articulate the preacher's ethos as crucial for their preaching experience. Form and content are inseparable. Speech cannot be separated from its speaker as a sermon cannot be separated from the preacher. This knowledge is as old as western culture, formulated already in antiquity by Aristotle:

> Of the modes of persuasion furnished by the spoken word there are three kinds. The first kind depends on the personal character of the speaker; the second on putting the audience into a certain frame of mind; the third on the proof, or apparent proof, provided by the words of the speech itself. Persuasion is achieved by the speaker's personal character when the speech is so spoken as to make us think him credible. We believe good men more fully and more readily than others: this is true generally whatever the question is, and absolutely true where exact certainty is impossible and opinions are divided.[17]

---

basic trust in God arising out of the awareness of belonging to God and participating in God's reality.

14. McClure et al., *Listening to Listeners*, 136–37, 142–44.
15. McClure, *Otherwise Thinking—A Blog*.
16. Fylling, *Hellige ord*, 77.
17. Aristotle, *Art of Rhetoric*, I, ch. 2, [1356a]. For a homiletical discussion of

Thus, Aristotle argues the character of the speaker—ethos—is the most authoritative, of the three modes of persuasion (logos, pathos and ethos). This notion has been supported by empirical studies in the twentieth century in communication theory.[18] And furthermore he writes:

> The orator persuades by moral character when his speech is delivered in such a manner as to render him worthy of confidence; for we feel confidence in a greater degree and more readily in persons of worth in regard to everything in general, but where there is no certainty and there is room for doubt, our confidence is absolute.[19]

According to Aristotle, there are three subcategories of ethos, named *phronesis* which is practical skills and wisdom, *arête* which is virtue and goodness, and *eunoia* which is goodwill towards the audience. The quality of *eunoia* is equivalent to the churchgoers' quest for a respectful, open attitude towards them. So, no wonder from a classical rhetorical point of view, the preacher's ethos is the main mode for preaching too.

Historically it is interesting to see how the role of ethos in the aftermath of the First World War (1914–18) has been problematized trough Neo-orthodoxy—in Europe often associated with dialectical theology.[20] For instance Karl Barth writes:

> those who are ministers have not to push their own interests, inclinations, convictions, and desires in what they do, nor serve the ideas and movements of their age, though they may also do this. Instead, they must see to it that by their actions it is clear that God has spoken and that God will speak. Where priority is thus given to the divine will and work over a human will and work, they will stand obediently in God's service and authentic Christian preaching will take place.[21]

rhetorical term "persuasion," see Hogan, "Rethinking Persuasion"; and Lischer, "Why I Am Not Persuasive."

18. McCroskey, "Ethos" in *Introduction to Rhetorical Communication*, 87.

19. Aristotle, *Eth. nic.* Book A, II, 4.

20. Primarily associated with Karl Barth (1886–1968), even though Barth himself emphatically rejected the term neo-orthodoxy; Friedrich Gogarten (1887–1967); Eduard Thurneysen (1888–1974); Rudolf Bultmann (1884–1976); Emil Brunner (1899–1966); and Reginald H. Fuller (1915–2007). It must be said that dialectical theology was formulated before the linguistic turn and its rejection of the transfer model. The Norwegian theologian Hognestad addresses Barth's understanding of language in his doctoral dissertation, see Hognestad, *Ordet i ordene*. He and writes in his conclusion, that Barth reduces language to be nothing more than a tool.

21. Barth, *Homiletics*, 69.

The Third Room of Preaching

The reaction against the nineteenth century liberal theology for what the dialectical theology perceived as "divinization of human thinking" also included a rejection of the ethos of the preacher's person in preaching which is quite unlike the earlier mentioned North American homiletican Phillips Brooks who said in a lecture in 1877, that peaching:

> has two essential elements, truth and personality. [...] The truth must come really through the person [...] his character, his affections, his whole intellectual and moral being.[22]

Consistent with the empirical perspective and beyond, the gospel is communicated through the preacher's ethos according to Brooks. But right up to the 1970s, whereas the concept of the Word of God has had a dominant influence in Protestant theology, the importance of the preacher's ethos has been perceived as problematic. According to dialectical theology, it is not the preacher who inspires faith, but God, who is *das ganz Andere*, totally distinct from and with no point of contact to human beings. At ordination pastors in Denmark sign a vow declaring, that they shall "preach the Word of God clean and pure."[23] Even though many interpretations have defined the preaching event differently from the Word of God tradition, the expression "the Word of God clean and pure" undoubtedly sustains the idea that the preacher can transfer the Word of God written in the Bible to the listeners without coloring the "Word" with their own biases. A more apt empirical expression, however, would be to preach the Word of God with personal engagement, integrity, and faith.

One of the big advantages of the influential North American movement known as the New Homiletic is that movement's increasing rejection of the implicit transfer model and of the attempt to identify new understandings of communication in preaching granting the listeners an active role in various ways. The sermon is understood as an interactive event encouraging the listeners to create meaning through the dynamic interplay between the preacher and the listeners. The sermon is no longer seen as an informative activity, transferring theological meaning from one consciousness to another, but as a performative discourse trying to do what it is saying. Embedded in this understanding of communication is an implicit anthropology seeing the listeners not as passive receivers of the message,

---

22. Brooks, *Lectures on Preaching*, 8.
23. The same is true for pastors in Norway.

but as active individuals who independently create meaning in the sermon they hear. But what is the preacher's role?

In the new millennium, the attention towards the preacher's authenticity in homiletic literature has increased as a modern ideal among preachers of being true to themselves.[24] The strong emphasis on personal dimension, according to the Canadian philosopher Charles Taylor can be interpreted as an expression of the demand for authenticity that characterizes late modern society.[25] Taylor writes that there it is a basic condition of late modernity that individual no longer can refer to an external authority as justification for their actions, but must ground it in their own convictions. Individualism is thus an indispensable part of the legacy of the Enlightenment.[26] For the pulpit it means that authenticity seems to have replaced the previous concept of authority, or that authority grows out of authenticity. Authentic preachers are not trying to eliminate themselves from the pulpit or present themselves as perfect, but seek rather to be transparent and to communicate from a genuine desire for self-knowledge, writes McClure.[27] There is a great awareness and practical understanding of the importance of the preacher's authenticity, but the theological explanation for *why* the preacher's authenticity is so crucial is relatively limited.

Yet, there are some different suggestions for the preacher's role, such as the witness who testifies what the preacher has heard and seen in the texts.[28] The storyteller invites the congregation to go on a journey similar to the one the preachers traveled to their own "Eureka" experiences.[29] The role of herald is a classic.[30] Another proposal comes from the North American homiletican Charles Campbell and the South African homiletican Johan Cilliers defining the preacher's role as the fool, characterized by humiliation, ridicule and weakness.[31] The preaching fool can disturb the traditional

---

24. This can be seen as consistent with the highly individualized understanding of the self in Western culture.

25. Taylor, *Modernitetens ubehag*, 70.

26. Reid, "Authenticity in Preaching."

27. McClure, *Preaching Words*, 6.

28. Long, *Witness of Preaching*; Florence, *Preaching as Testimony*.

29. Craddock, *As One Without Authority*.

30. The herald as a recurring metaphor is found in many pieces of dialectic inspired homiletics literature. For diverse images of the preacher's role, see Reid, *Slow of Speech and Unclean Lips*. The book is based on a panel discussion at the Academy of Homiletics, where eight scholars of preaching propose and explain their different images.

31. Cambell and Cilliers, *Preaching Fools*, 32.

way of thinking, but has no control over the communication situation. They argue that the fool undermines the classical rhetorical understanding of the preacher's ethos. In this book the idea that the preacher has no power to control the communication process is supported by the empirical findings from the perspective of the pew, but not the idea that preaching is experienced as disturbance or disruption. Nor do authors put forth empirical evidence supporting the idea that preacher'srole is perceived as the fool's. Rather the listeners respect the preacher, if they perceive him or her as authentic. But the congregation's request for authenticity is still to be investigated and explained theologically.

The traditional Protestant theological conviction ascribes an inherent religious function to preaching, and both a Reformed and a Lutheran theology consider preaching as a united human and divine agency. The challenge is still to explain how agency in preaching can be both personal and relational constituted in accordance with the empirical experience (the quest for authenticity), and at the same time consistent with a theology of preaching perceiving God as the one inspiring faith. How can we theologically explain why the personal relationship with the preacher affects the listeners' interaction with the sermon? And how are we to understand the united agency in preaching, and what are the homiletic consequences? The theological question of why authenticity, including personal faith, is essential for the listeners remains to be answered.

John McClure outlines four different theologies of preaching:[32] an *existential*, a *transcendent*, an *ethical-political*, and an *organic-aesthetic* theology. The *existential* theology supplies a divine Word that answers a crisis or conflict at the heart of human existence (represented by, for example, Paul Tillich). In the *transcendent* theology we have to rely utterly on the divine Word in the Bible, and in the Christ witnessed to in Scripture, independently of human experiences[33] (represented by for example Karl Barth).[34] The *ethical-political* theology perceives the divine Word as an

---

32. McClure, *Preaching Words*, 136–40.

33. McClure writes: "This transcendent model and the existential model are typically in great tension with each other. In today's homiletic context, this tension takes the shape of the debate between the liberal New Homiletic and postliberal homiletics debate" (*Preaching Words*, 138).

34. However, as I said previously, it is worth noting that Karl Bart's dialectical theology was formulated before the linguistic turn and the rejection of the transfer model.

alternate vision to injustice, inequities of power, suffering, and oppression (represented by liberation theology, black theology, or feminist theology).[35]

The way McClure presents these three preaching theologies, they do not account for *why* the person and the relation are so important in preaching. Despite the briefly explained differences, the common approach for these theologies are that they do *not* take into account our own *participation* in the world, thus it is impossible to say something about the divine Word independent of our own being. As explained in chapter 2, this involves a paradigmatic shift from understanding the Divine Word as an ontological category, to an epistemological consciousness in which The Word of God as independent and external substantial category breaks down.

The fourth preaching theology is the *organic-aesthetic* theology, in which the divine Word is always available deep within the *organic interconnectedness of all living things* (represented by for example Marjorie Suchocki and I could add, the Danish philosopher Dorthe Jørgensen). This understanding can be found in process-relational theologians who are convinced that everything is dynamically interconnected, that everything matters, that everything has an effect, and that God is the most relational reality of all.[36] A similar understanding can also be found in Scandinavian Creation Theology believing that we all live in networks of deep *interdependence*.[37] The notion of all living creatures' interdependence or interconnectedness can be a gateway to a theological interpretation of why the preacher and the relation is so important for the listeners' preaching event.

Another interpretation key can be the Danish philosopher Søren Kierkegaard who stress the need for the preacher's authenticity. He argues that the non-authentic preacher perceives himself as the master of Christianity rather than the servant. The problem according to Kierkegaard is the human desire for securing ourselves, rather than being obedient to God. The preacher's authenticity grows out of being obedient to God, and in the willingness to surrender oneself to God, in which the human cannot control or secure oneself. Therefore the preacher's relationship with God is reflected in the preacher's authenticity. This is in line with the empirical findings of the listeners' request for the preacher's authenticity including

---

35. The ethical-political theology is not highly presented in the traditional Danish folk church primarily consisting of a homogenous ethnic Danes, but much more in migrant churches.

36. McClure, *Preaching Words*, 139–40.

37. See for example Gregersen et al., *Reformation Theology*.

being faithful to own faith—which affects the interaction of the congregation with the sermon. This points towards the next category emerging from the analysis, the relationship between listener and preacher which sets the context in which the words of the sermon are interpreted.

3.2 THE RECIPROCAL RELATIONSHIP BETWEEN LISTENER AND PREACHER

> I can tell when the preacher puts himself at stake and is touched by the texts—then I'm also touched and dare to put myself at stake.[38]

The personal engagement of the authentic preacher seems to activate and stimulate the listener's interaction with the text and the sermon, and thereby the preacher's faith influences the churchgoers' outcome of the preaching event. This relationship was not the only criterion to influence the listeners, but it was one of the important ones. There was a tendency that the listeners were touched and moved, when they experienced that the preacher was touched and moved by the text. The preacher is "a tool" for the gospel, so to speak, which can affect and inspire the listeners. This implies that the preacher's relation to the gospel and ultimately her or his relationship with God inspires and affects the listeners' interaction with the sermon. So there is a kind of reciprocity in the relationship between the preacher, the listeners and the gospel, emerging in the preaching and listening event. This phenomenon I have called *the reciprocal relation*.

So, the interaction and the outcome of the sermon is dependent on the reciprocal relational environment in which the listening and preaching event takes place, and thus the interaction is far more than the cognitive reception of words and the semantic content of the sermon. Also an emotional, and I would add a spiritual, dimension is emerging in the situation. When the pastor in the eyes of the churchgoers is open, engaged, exposing herself and believes in her own words, the listeners are more willing to be accompanied and directed in new directions moving away from their starting point:

> I think it's really great that she as a preacher uses herself in the sermon... it's as if... (pause) at least it touches me more, I think. [39]

---

38. Female listener to a radio broadcast of a service of worship.
39. 63-year-old female churchgoer.

Opposite, if the pastor is perceived as personally closed, absent, absorbed in her manuscript and without contact to the congregation or herself, then the churchgoers are more inclined to stop paying attention, or to put it in other words, to withdraw from the reciprocal relationship. The listeners' interpretations of the preacher's words are shaped in the reciprocal relationship where something can block the interaction, so the communication process is not working appropriately. If one of the participants is closed or not present, it may block the relationship.

For many churchgoers there was a parallel between being able to "feel" the preacher and the benefit of the sermon. The experience of an authentic preacher activates an authentic dialogic response in the listeners. Therefore, the experience of the preacher's attitude, authenticity and faith is essential for churchgoers. This may seem obvious, for why be present in a relation if the other is absent? If the preaching event is understood as an encounter between the preacher's outer words and the listener's inner experiences facilitating a third room, then it requires that the participants are open and present in the relationship.

It is remarkable, however, that the opposite is also the case from the perspective of the pulpit. The interviews with the pastors showed, that when the congregation is perceived as noisy, uninterested, absent, or just more attentive to their cell phones than the worship, then the preachers are affected. They become absent, unfocused and preach in a more mechanical way. In reverse an attentive and committed congregation is experienced as stimulating the preacher's presence and engagement in the pulpit. As the worshipers wanted an attentive and engaged preacher, so the preachers appreciated an attentively listening congregation. The influence of one and another in the relationship is reciprocal. This is probably a phenomenon that most people—both preachers and churchgoers—recognize from their experience, but how are we to understand theologically the human reciprocal relationship in the preaching event in relation to the divine agency?

Something More

> I know (the pastor) well, and then you are very *open* and receptive. I think she is a lovely person who really invites you to listen to her and like her.[40]

---

40. 46-year-old female churchgoer (my italics).

The Third Room of Preaching

The churchgoers typically used verbs like "open," "receive," or "close," "get off," indicating a sensory perception rather than only a cognitive reception of the preacher's words, when they were asked to respond to the sermon and actually responded to the preacher. I interpret utterances like the ones above as an emphasis of the sensory perception of the sermon. A precondition for this perception is for listener and preacher to be *open*.

The preaching event can thus be understood as an interaction having the character of an open encounter between active participants in a communication process, in which mutual influence is possible. If we take seriously that the empirical experience of preaching from both the perspective of the pew and the pulpit is much more than the cognitive and intellectual content of the preacher's words, but also is sensing and interacting with the other in the reciprocal relationship which implies that the participants are open and in contact with each other, it could be that the appreciation of being *open* also implies being open to interact with, or even participate, in the divine agency in preaching.

The interviews, however, testified that the preacher cannot control or determine whether, or to what extent, or in which direction the listeners are moved, if they are moved at all. The preachers can move the listeners (maybe—since there is no guarantee) by investing themselves, putting themselves at risk, by being open, and by sharing their experience of the encounter with the gospel, and by showing what or how the text in their eyes interprets contemporary life. However, these things should not be confused with their ability to control the interaction of the communication process, or with having the power to move the listeners in a specific direction. Thus, the analysis indicated that the listener is dependent upon the external words of the preacher in order to create meaning, but the listeners' meanings are not necessarily identical with the preacher's intention. The preacher is characterized by not having the power to control the communication process, but I will argue, it does not remove the preacher's responsibility to contribute to that process. One can advantageously distinguish between *power* and *responsibility*: The preacher does not have power to control how the listener understands and interprets the words, but the preachers are in charge of designing the sermon in accordance with their faith and belief as clearly and focused as possible. The communication process in the preaching event is more like a dynamic and vibrant relationship in which the listeners are activated by the preacher's words, sometimes in quite unpredictable and surprising ways. Something more is at work.

Evidently preaching is more than the rational and semantic meaning attached to the words of the sermon. There is also a non-cognitive interaction at stake, which may move the focus from words to spirit. According to my empirical findings, preaching is to be understood as a relational defined interaction in which the listeners are inspired by the preacher's investment in the relationship, and the preacher is dependent on the listeners' attention, thus the preacher and congregation are mutually reliant on each other. The preacher's presence and authenticity are influenced by the churchgoers' willingness to listen and interact with the sermon, at the same time, the churchgoers' willingness to listen to and interact with the sermon is influenced by the preacher's authenticity and presence. Thus, the notion of the reciprocal relation is here, but as mentioned earlier, something more is at work. When the preacher is affected and moved by the gospel, it affects the churchgoers. The gospel indirectly represents a third agency in the relationship. This is important, and points toward the Third Room of Preaching, to which I shall return in section 3.6.

Focus in the analysis here is circling around the participants—the listener and the preacher—in the preaching event, but, of course, also in the liturgical context, the church room with the rest of the congregation, prayers, hymns, singing, organ playing, candles, Eucharist, baptism, maybe a crucifix at the altar or Christian paintings. The entire worship service is present and influential in the preaching event and is essential for the listeners' interaction with the sermon. The words of the sermon would probably sound different, if they were preached in a totally different context—for instance in a mall, at a soccer stadium, or a railway station. Being in a church has connotation to that specific room—*the witnessing of faith throughout history*. The experiences the individual relates to that room, the feelings and memories it activates, and the fact that the churchgoers have decided to go to church, set the frames for the way the listeners hear, understand and interpret the sermon. (For instance, if they hear about a woman suffering of discharge of blood, the first thought is certainly not that this description is part of an advertisement for sanitary napkins.) Going into a church Sunday morning sets the mind and shapes the expectation for what is going to happen, and this obviously participates in forming the preaching event. However, this does not overrule the empirical finding, that the reciprocal relationship is essential for the listeners' preaching interaction.

The Third Room of Preaching

The Reciprocal Relation in Dialogue with Theoretical and Theological Considerations

There are several things that call for a more detailed theoretical and theological reflection in the interpretation of the empirical finding of the reciprocal relation. First, the preaching event has to be understood not only in relation to the preacher's words or manuscript, but also in relation to the relation of the participants to the preacher's words. Next, the shift from the semantic meaning related to the words of the sermon to the sensory perception, indicating a shift in focus from logos to spirit needs to be investigated. What does it mean theologically that the semantic meaning usually attached to the words alone, cannot be separated from the person using the words and the relation in which the words are interpreted? And what does it mean that the preaching event cannot be separated from the worship situation, in which it is embedded?[41] Thus, I continued to search for a communication theology and theory to illuminate the reciprocal dimension of the preaching situation.

To consider communication as intertwined with subjectivity and relations has been in the forefront of communication theories in recent decades, and this thinking is also reflected in theology. The former archbishop in South Africa, Desmond Tutu, describes the reciprocal relationship between people with an African concept of *ubuntu*. Tutu writes:

> We live in a web of interdependence with our fellow human beings and with the rest of God's creatures. In Africa, the realization of our interdependence is called *ubuntu* [...] It is the essence of being human. It is the fact, that my humanity is inextricably entangled with your humanity. I am a human because I am related. [...] It has something to do with what it means to be truly human, to know that you are connected with others in a network of life.[42]

The South African homiletician Johan Cilliers defines *ubuntu* this way: "In short it means: humanity, or humanness. It stems from the belief that one is a human being through others—"I am because you are." [43] In English, German, Spanish, French, Latin (or for my part Danish), the

---

41. This idea is thought-provoking in a Danish context, in which many sermon collectionss are published: preaching from an empirical point of view cannot be separated from the situation in which it is embedded. Printing the sermon without the situation affects the way the reader interprets the words.

42. Tutu, *Gud har en drøm*, 34–35.

43. Cilliers, "In Search of Meaning," 74.

language that carries our theological tradition, there is no word semantically identical with the concept of *ubuntu*, a word that describes the essence of being human. Cilliers elaborates the definition:

> *Ubuntu* rather defines the individual in terms of relationships. It represents a sort of web of reciprocal relations in which subject and object are indistinguishable. Therefore not: "I think, therefore I am," but rather "I participate, therefore I am."[44]

If the traditional hermetic distinction between subject and object is repealed, and instead, the focus moves from individual to relationship, then the underlying assumption in the process of communication has to be redefined in preaching theology. It means that the individual cannot be defined without the concept of the others. Individualism is informed by collectivity, and autonomy cannot be defined without the concept of community. Solitude is part of sociality. The notion of the self cannot be understood without the relation in which the self participates. If we, as an extension to the traditional understanding of the self, perceive the self as the intersecting node where many relations meet, we may realize how these relations define the self, and these relations influence the way the self understands and creates meaning in communication with others. This understanding of the self is the foundation of the social constructionist.[45] Social constructionism communication theory examines the development of jointly constructed understandings of the world that form the basis for shared assumptions about reality. The theory centers on the notions that human beings rationalize their experience by creating models of the social world and share and reify these models through language. My intention, however, is not to argue for the social constructionist or any other particular communication theory, but my hope is to find theories helping to elucidate and explain the empirical finding that the relationship between the listener and the preacher sets the context in which the words of the sermon are interpreted—the reciprocal relationship.

---

44. Cilliers, "In Search of Meaning," 79.

45. For instance, Kenneth Gergen, an American psychologist associated with social constructionism, argues in his book, *Realities and Relationships,* that western culture through centuries has placed the individual at the center of knowledge. If we instead consider individualized concepts (such as faith and doubt) as discursive processes, since individuals are dependent on others for discursive practices, we are compelled to transfer our conception of the individual as center of human knowledge, to an understanding which centralizes social relationships carried out in language. This position will be elaborated later in section 3.5.

An understandable and common reaction to the imperial result is questioning. Is it is possible to maintain both the empirical demand for authenticity, acknowledge the importance of the reciprocal relation, and at the same time avoid a (too) strong focus on the preacher's person (for God does not show favoritism),[46] and understand preaching as a divine enterprise? My answer is yes. What at first glance may seem like an *overload* of ecclesial ministry and the person on the pulpit, can also be interpreted as a *relief* for the preacher him or herself. It requires, however, a redefinition of some of the sub assumptions associated with the theological understanding of the communication process in preaching. The understanding of communication as a transfer of meaning, the so-called transfer model, must be replaced with another more adequate understanding of communication allowing the person and the relationship between the participants a greater latitude. This will be elaborated theoretically in next step of the presentation of the main results of the empirical analysis, concerning the dialogical ways the listeners interact with the sermon and create meaning.

3.3 LISTENING TO PREACHING AS AN INTERNAL DIALOGUE[47]

> (Listening to preaching) is like descending into a sort of a reflexive room, which is a dialogue with what is happening in the worship service [...] and why should I be part of that dialogue if the one who, communicating the message, cannot even vouch for it, or is speaking from his heart.[48]

Although, preaching from a phenomenal perspective appears to be a monologue—one preacher speaking to a silent listening congregation—the experience from the listener's perspective can be described as an internal dialogue in which the outer voice of the preacher is only one among other voices for the listener. Many preachers will probably recognize the experience of someone in the congregation referring to something in the sermon, which the preacher for sure knows that he or she has not said. Even though the congregation from an outside perspective is silently listening, their minds are not silent—they are busy, full of words and thoughts. From this

---

46. Rom 2:11 (NRSV)

47. The different kinds of dialogical interaction are also presented in Gaarden and Lorensen, "Listeners as Authors in Preaching."

48. 53-year-old female churchgoer, working as a professor.

point of view the sermon can be described as an internal dialogue activated by the external words of the sermon.

The voice of the preacher is like an implicit interlocutor and theological reflector activating thoughts in the minds of the listeners. The preacher is important for the listener, because the listener allows the preacher's voice to interfere with their private thoughts and beliefs. The following quotation, from a churchgoer who participated in a service in a prison church where the culture is less controlled and formalized, did not refrain from entering into explicit dialogue.

> I tell her (the preacher), if I disagree with her. Then I interrupt the sermon by saying 'It's not quite right', and then she tries to convince me. [...] Sometimes we wildly disagree, but then you would have heard! [...] I would have opposed her.[49]

In this way, the listener also indicates that the listening process is activating a dialogue, even though he did not use the word dialogue. He was simply blunter and would interrupt the sermon and turn it into an explicit dialogue, if he disagreed with the preacher whom he actually appreciated highly. The utterances of these two listeners, representing two different cultures, backgrounds, and contexts—a professor and an inmate—reveal a consistent feature in the interviews: That listening to the preacher's voice activates, at a cognitive level, the churchgoer's personal flow of thoughts, which in different ways is triggered by the dialogical interaction with the sermon.

Even though the congregation's focus apparently is directed towards the preacher's person, who is evaluated according to how the listener experiences the preacher, then the decisive element for the listener's preaching event *is not the preacher him- or herself, but the internal dialogue* that the preacher facilities. When the churchgoers are asked what they have heard in a sermon, they express what they have been thinking in relation to the fragments of the sermon they actually had heard. Usually the listeners' minds are activated by small fragments of the sermon they process, and they reflect on these fragments that are left in their minds. What the preacher actually has said in the pulpit is entirely interwoven with the listener's own thoughts, reflections, and believes. So the churchgoers' experiences of the sermon are completely interwoven with, and inseparable from, their own thoughts in dialogue with the sermon. It is, therefore, almost impossible to

---

49. 66-year-old male churchgoer, inmate in an open state prison.

disentangle what the listener has heard and what the preacher actually has said. The *listener's inner sermon* is the dialogical response to the actually spoken sermon. Often the content and the semantic meaning of the inner sermon is not in accordance with preacher's intention, and the creativity of the dialogical interaction is so profound that it appears as a different—and sometimes even totally divergent—discourse compared to the one held by the preacher. There are as many sermons in the church as there are people present.

> I experience listening as a dialogue with the different elements (of the worship service) which cause me think about, and reflect upon my life right here and now, or upon some more existential issues.[50]

The words of the sermon are processed, contextualized and adjusted to the listeners' own life experiences, preunderstandings, and beliefs. Often the preacher's words participate in an already existing inner dialogue about issues, problems, joys, or sorrows which the churchgoers bring with them into church. Thus, the churchgoers' benefits from the sermon arises from the dialogical way they interact with the sermon and the entire worship service, and their inner sermons are the activated thoughts and reflection based on their personal lives. To put it simply, there are as many sermons, as there are churchgoers.

During the analysis, however, a distinction of the listeners' approach to the internal dialogue emerged. Some listeners were *confirmed* and some were *moved* by the preacher's words. For some the churchgoers the sermon supports their theologies and world views when the sermon confirms their pre-understandings. Indeed, I found a tendency in the data for those listeners to base their internal dialogues upon ideological pre-conceptions that brought with them to the sermon. Some even based their dialogues upon what they had learned as children in Sunday School. These listeners tended to hear the sermon as confirming their pre-existing notions. While the majority of churchgoers I interviewed were *moved* by the preacher's words, these listeners based their internal dialogue upon their own experiences, and related their understanding of the sermon to issues and challenges in their real life. The dialogue with the sermon moved the listeners so as to give rise to new interpretations or new perspectives of their life experiences.

---

50. 53-year-old female churchgoer.

Exploring the Third Room in Preaching

The Dialogical Interaction in Dialogue with Theoretical and Theological Considerations

Barbara Brown Tayler, touches briefly on one of the reasons that listening to preaching is actually a dialogical response, when she writes:

> While most human beings speak at a rate of one hundred twenty to one hundred fifty words a minute, we can process more than five hundred words a minute, which makes it hard for us to say tuned to prolonged communication, especially if the speaker is halting or dull. We tend to use the lag time in a conversation to compose our own responses.[51]

That listening to sermons from an empirical point of view is formed by a dialogical response resonates deeply with the Russian dialogue philosopher, Mikhail Bakhtin's epistemological theories that can illuminate and explain some of the empirical results of this study.[52] According to Bakhtin, recognition and understanding only emerge as a response to the other's external words. Reasoning and response are dialectically linked and mutually interdepended of each other in a way that one is impossible without the other. Dialogue is crucial, not only to human communication but also to human processes of reasoning and understanding according to Bakhtin. Rather than seeing dialogue as a pedagogical product based on individual thinking, dialogical interaction and the words of others provide the epistemological foundation for creative thinking and the development of individuals.[53] Dialogue is constitutive for all human reasoning and understanding. All reasoning is formed by a dialogical response. Or to put it another way, the dialogical interaction with external words are the epistemological foundation for all creative thinking, and growth of human beings.[54]

This resonates deeply with the empirical findings highlighting the idea that listeners' understandings come to fruition in the dialogical response

---

51. Taylor, *When God is Silent*, 14–15.

52. I am indebted to my Danish colleague, professor in practical theology at Copenhagen University, Marlene Ringgaard Lorensen, for inspiring discussions and collaborative work. Together with Lorensen, who investigated in her doctoral dissertation Mikhail Bakhtin's theoretical approach to dialogicity in relation to preaching, *Dialogical Preaching*, we have analyzed the empirical findings in the light of Bakhtin's theory in the article "Listeners as Authors."

53. Bakhtin, *Speech Genres*, 67–68.

54. Gaarden and Lorensen, "Listeners as Authors," 31–32.

to the sermon. In line with the churchgoers' descriptions of their implicit dialogue, Bakhtin highlights the valuable significance of the other's outside perspective for human communication and understanding. Rather than trying to understand the other's different point of view through empathic identification, then it is more fruitful to encounter the other as a dialogue partner whose different perspective can bring a new dimension of understanding into the dialogue. The profoundness and significance of a point of view only becomes apparent when it encounters a different point of view. Two positions can enter into a dialogue without resulting in a synthesis or fusion of meanings, and each retains its own entity, but mutually enriches the other.

Bakhtin's analysis of the importance of the other's outside and different perspective is developed as a critique of the epistemology that assumes that total identification between two persons is possible—or even desirable. A productive dialogue does not require complete identification between the participants, rather it requires respect for, and not reducing, the different perspectives. According to Bakhtin it will never be possible to see one's own understanding totally reflected in the other's understanding, as it would require that one could shape the other in his or her own image which is neither possible nor desirable. One could even argue that shaping the other in one's own image is a modified form of idolatry. What could be obtained by merging the other's perspective with one's own other than just a clone of oneself? That would just be a repetition of one's own life and understandings. Because of her or his outer perspective, the other may be able to see what we cannot see from our own points of view. Thus, the other's external perspective can enrich and add new dimensions to our lives. The different perspectives can be seen as a constructive distance, because it includes a surplus of positions which create opportunity for new creative understandings. New insight and understanding are therefore not determined by identification between two positions, rather new insight comes from distance and diversity.[55]

Bakhtin distinguishes between monological and dialogical understandings. In the monological understanding the other's words are just used as a scaffold for one's own thoughts; nothing new is added, while the dialogical understanding allows the other's words to influence and transform the architecture of one's own thinking. According to Bakhtin, the successful communication is therefore dependent on a strong, flexible (and I

---

55. Gaarden and Lorensen, "Listeners as Authors," 33.

could add reciprocal) relationship between the other and me. To keep the relationship open and flexible, interaction with—and respecting the perspective of the other—are important.

The determining difference between monological and dialogical approaches depends on whether the words of the other are allowed to transform the architecture of the self, or whether they are used simply as scaffolding. In the latter case, monologue might contribute bits and pieces to one's own development but are not allowed to have a lasting impact on the discourse itself.

Bakhtin's distinction between monological and dialogical understanding corresponds to the analysis of empirical data in this study by showing that the preacher's words either influence the architecture of the churchgoers thinking and beliefs, or simply serve as scaffolding for the listeners' pre-understandings. As mentioned, some churchgoers were just confirmed in what they already knew, while others—the majority—were moved by the preacher's words. A new dimension or new perspective was added to their pre-understandings. According to Bakhtin, these churchgoers allow the sermon to affect and influence the architecture of their understanding trough different kinds of dialogical interaction, so that new understandings can occur. Often the interviewees expressed, that the "new understanding" was a reminder of what they actually already knew, but had forgotten.[56] Yet, even if they had perceived something before but had forgotten it, it returned to them with the partial force of something new and something recovered.

In light of Bakhtin's emphasis on dialogue as crucial to processes of understanding, the listeners' focus on the preacher makes sense. Preaching is not a one-way transfer from an active speaker to passive absorbing listeners. The words of the preacher's manuscript need not remain in the minds of the churchgoers, but the important thing is that their own dialogical interaction take place, based on their existential and religious reflections, and current life situations. This understanding of communication challenges many traditional homiletical assumptions which exclusively consider the preacher to have *the ownership* of the sermon. Rather a communication theology based on dialogical interaction needs to be elaborated and integrated in a contemporary homiletic. This new synthesis includes the crucial

---

56. Gaarden and Lorensen, "Listeners as Authors," 32; Bakhtin, *Problems of Dostoevsky's Poetics*, 187.

question of how are we to understand the relationship between human-divine agency in preaching.

What at first glance might seem like an exaggerated focus on the preacher's person and an overload on the pastoral office, may at a closer look turn out to be *a relief for the preacher*. I interpret the dialogical way of listening and reasoning as one of the big reasons for why the listeners grant the preacher's authenticity and attitude such a big significance. The preacher, who at first glance appears to be so central for churchgoers, is in fact *only the facilitator* for the real essential—namely the internal dialogue. It is important to highlight that the preacher is only participating in facilitating this interactive event as other factors in the entire worship participate too, such as other churchgoers, hymns and singing, the church building, prayers and readings, the liturgy with the Eucharist, Baptism, etc. Yet, for the preacher to be open, and to have an appreciative and respectful attitude towards the other, is important for the entire situation in which preaching takes place. And the preacher who is authentic, engaged, and faithful towards the gospel invites the listeners to a reciprocal authentic, engaged, and faithful dialogical interaction. From an empirical point of view, the congregations' internal dialogues *cannot be controlled* by the preacher's intentions. The preacher does not have this power even though the preacher plays a crucial role as the facilitator and as such is responsible for the sermon, Therefore, it is *not the preacher per se*, but the dialogical *interaction* which is at the core of the preaching event.

Martin Luther, the initiator of the Protestant Reformation, understands the worship service as a dialogue between God and human. For Luther it is important that it is not the human who serves God in the worship service, but God serves humans. Luther defined worship as "nothing else" need ever happen "except that our dear Lord himself may speak to us through his holy Word and we respond to him through prayer and praise."[57] Through the outer words of the gospel (Latin *verbum externum*) arises faith in the inner heart (Latin *verbum internum*) giving human a new destination and transform human in the world.[58] Thus, the worship service is a dialogue between God and human beings.

---

57. Martin Luther first formulated this definition in a "Sermon at the Dedication of the Castle Church in Torgau" (1544), in *Weimarer Ausgabe* 49, often abbreviated WA 49. The official title is *D. Martin Luthers Werke: Kritische Gesammtausgabe*.

58. WA 39/1, 492, 3.

If we accept the empirical findings of this study, this dialogical interaction is facilitated but not controlled by any of the participants. My interpretation points to a liminal space emerging in the preaching event where the *listeners' inner experiences encounter the outer words of the sermon*. According to the Danish theologian N.F.S. Grundtvig, the living word of the gospel takes place in that space between pulpit and pew.[59] Christ is found in the living community rather than in the Bible or in any book. From his point of view, congregational and sacramental Christianity are the substitution of the authority of the living Word of God. Could it be that this empirically evident internal dialogue can be understood as the living Word of God? And that this internal dialogue, as the living Word dependent upon, but not controlled by, the participants is mastered by the divine agency? I was curious, and continued to investigate empirical dialogical interaction more deeply. It should be mentioned here, before continuing to the more profound analysis of the dialogical interaction of the interviews, that some of the contemporary homiletical literature operates with a dialogical approach to preaching.[60]

Three Kinds of Dialogical Interaction

This dialogue can best be described as a polyphony of *voices* interwoven in the listening process. In this polyphony, the perspectives often shifted, which can be illustrated by this churchgoer's semantic interrupted utterance:

> I've heard this before in relation to other texts that you have to take care of your neighbor. Well, I found the text interesting, because it is commonly known... or at least the idea of a poor life on Earth is a ticket to Heaven... but this perspective has also been used politically against Christianity.... But we can, all of us and the church as well, try to be better persons and live in accordance with the essence of faith.[61]

---

59. Nikolai Frederik Severin Grundtvig (1783–1872), normally referred to as N. F. S. Grundtvig, a pastor, author, poet, philosopher, historian, teacher and politician, was one of the most influential people in Danish history and considered one of the founding fathers of the nation. For an introduction to Grundtvig's influence and thinking see Allchin, *N. F. S. Grundtvig*, and Gregersen, *Human Comes First*.

60. As an example of this literature, see Allen and Allen, *Sermon Without End*. Allen and Allen offer an informative and reader-friendly overview of homiletical literature in Eurocentric circles with a "postapologetic, conversational spirit at work," Allen and Allen, *Sermon Without End*, 108–14.

61. 63-year-old man working as a journalist.

This churchgoer moved quickly through a chain of associations in dialogue with only a little fragment of the sermon: "Take care of your neighbor." Initially, he identified the topic of the sermon, put the theme in relation to other texts, then he evaluated the text, continued to consider the effect the text has had in history, and subsequently he interpreted the text in his own way, concluding what the church and the congregation ought to do. This chain of association can be described as a polyphony of voices, through which he had a dialogue with the text, the preacher's interpretation of the text, other persons' interpretations of the text, and the effects the text has had in history and in relation to his own context.

Three categories abductively emerged during the analysis of this polyphonic dialogue. These can be defined as an *associative*, *critical*, and *contemplative* interaction with the preacher's words.[62] Unlike the first two categories, the last one was less or even totally non-cognitive and therefore more difficult to identify in the interviews. The first two categories were the most frequent, and both the interaction of the listeners who were *confirmed* and those how were *moved* by the preacher's words could be subsumed in the two categories, the associative and critical. The third category, the contemplative mode, I will interpret as being able to move the listeners as well, but as this interaction transcends words and thoughts, it is more the clear traces and signs of results of this contemplative modus which can be identified in the interviews—such as the interviewees talking about the feeling of inner peace and serenity after the worship service. Although the categories here are listed as three separate categories, they rarely appeared isolated in the interviews. More often they dynamically overlapped. Thus, the churchgoer could move from being associative to critical and then back again to the associative mode again or suddenly jump into the contemplative modus.

The Associative Interaction

> Well, when I listen to the sermons, it is a combination of listening and thinking. I hear something, and if it really affects me or has an impact on something which I'm already occupied with [...] then I continue to elaborate on it for a while by going on another path

---

62. In a Norwegian research project investigating how children and young people interact with sermons, the three categories are also found. The study is forthcoming as Kaufman, *Mer enn ord*. See also Kaufman and Mosdøl, "More Than Words."

for myself. That's fine. And then I come back thinking, 'where are we now'?[63]

The associative way of reasoning in the analysis is the most frequent and the easiest to identify. The encounter with the preacher's external words activated a chain of inner associations. In this chain of associative thoughts, the churchgoers relate fragments of the sermon to their own life experiences and preunderstandings in order to make coherence and meaning in what they have heard. Often the listeners' thoughts move in their own tracks:

> When you are listening, you get derailed in a way, and then suddenly your get caught by what is said [...] then your thoughts rush away, and in a moment you are inattentive to what has been said—and then you form your own version.[64]

The two churchgoers express a central characteristic of all the interviews: It is the churchgoers' personal thoughts that matter, and they refer to their associative reflections, considerations, and evaluations in dialogue with the parts of the sermon they have actually heard. The listeners constructed understanding and meaning by means of association. Often the churchgoers' associations were stimulated by only one or a few fragments of the sermon—an image or a sentence—which activated the association's chain. What they remembered was the association and the meaning they have created in the dialogue with the sermon—sometimes far from the semantic contents of the actual held sermon. The listeners bring their own life situation with them into the church building, and their concerns cannot be separated from the sermon or the entire worship. The listeners referred to the preacher's words only to a small extent.

An interesting feature of the associative interaction is the churchgoers' ability and inclination to create questions in dialogue with the sermon—even though that process is not the preacher's intention. The preacher's external words encourage and inspire the listeners by means of creative association to formulate personal questions. Thus, the listener identifies not answers but questions in the listening process. The preacher may offer an answer to a question which the preacher him or herself has found in the text. Nevertheless, the listeners do not simply take over the preacher's answer, but use the preacher's personal dialogue with the gospel to identify their own questions, and then they find their answers to these questions, as

---

63. 53-year-old female churchgoer, who worked as a professor.
64. The 66-year-old man who worshiped in prison.

illustrated by this churchgoer who explained that he attended worship service to be refilled. When I asked him what he was filled with, I expected him to say spirit, joy, peace or maybe inspiration. Instead, he answered "Questions!" He elaborated by explaining that the questions he had from church, he could not have asked himself, and they would not have appeared in his mind by reading newspapers or watching television. What the churchgoer received and brought with him was not the preacher's understanding of the gospel, but his own questions:

> I feel very much that when I myself recognize and formulate the questions, then the following week is characterized by the search for the answers. The questions are constantly in my thoughts. I see the questions in different places, and hopefully I will find—and indeed I do very often—the answers to the questions during the week. [...] Therefore, the sermon most of all activates me [...] causing me to seek answers.[65]

In this prominent way, the churchgoer demonstrated from an empirical perspective how the gospel is heard and received, namely as an implicit dialogue, encouraging the listener to seek answers. The churchgoer's struggle to create meaning and understanding was not limited to the worship service but can be described as *an ongoing search for meaning*. The search for meaning was a common feature in the interviewees' explanation of how they, in similar ways, transformed the preacher's clearly formulated message into new questions, leading to new associations and attempts to answer the listener's own questions. Thus, the churchgoer in an associative way uses the dialogue with the sermon to formulate questions, regardless of whether the listener understands, accepts, or adopts the preacher's point of view. The internal sermonic dialogue continues in the listener's consciousness after the worship service, and the listeners even take these questions with them into the coming week. Consequently, the listener's dialogue is not limited to the preaching event and the liturgical setting of the worship service, but it is fostered and activated by those things.

This empirical description of the on-going dialogical interaction is not consistent with the Christian existential understanding of preaching as *a moment* of personal decision leading the churchgoers to either a rejection or reception of the gospel.[66] Rather, preaching from an empirical point of

---

65. A 44-year-old male churchgoer, a professor of art and father of a child who was baptized.

66. Christian existentialism is often traced back to the work of the Danish philosopher

view is a far more dynamic process, activating a series of associations in a search for personal meaning in relation to the listener's life and experiences. Here in the middle of the interaction new evangelical horizons of understanding can be incarnated in the listener's life and can proceed through an internal dialogue. Seen through the empirical glasses the transformative element of preaching is neither the preacher nor the listener or the gospel per se but is the dialogical interaction. Focus moves from the words of the sermon and the listeners' reception, and points, instead, toward third room between the two participants in the preaching event—the dialogical interaction which can be formed in various ways.

Critical Interaction

> Sometimes I move into another story about how the text actually is supposed to be understood. Sometimes I feel it as if I am in contact with those who wrote it (and it is as if they are saying) 'Hey listen, maybe this is what the text says, but that's not how it should be understood'. And then I'm in the middle of an interpretation process.[67]

If the listeners do not understand or agree with the preacher's interpretation of the text, it prompts the listeners to formulate their own understandings and interpretations of the text as critical responses which I name the *critical interaction*. Thus, when the preacher's words clash with the listeners' pre-understandings, then the listening process is formulated as an objection, and takes the form of an implicit critical dialogue. The internal objection activates a search for alternative understanding and meaning. So in line with Bakhtin's epistemology, the listeners never completely are able to identify or empathize with the speaker's outside perspective, which is indeed is the case for the churchgoers and the preacher. This theoretical explanation is fully documented by the empirical findings and emphasized in the *critical voice*, typically expressed in the interviews as, "The preacher said…but I think…," and then the interviewees refer to their own inner critical responses, generated by their encounter with the outer words of the sermon.

---

and theologian, Søren Kierkegaard (1813–1855), who proposed that each person must make independent choices, which then constitute that person's existence. Another figure often associated with existentialism is the German theologian, Rudolph Bultmann (1884–1976), arguing that faith must be a determined and vital act of will.

67. A 46-year-old male in the prison church.

In this way the preacher's different perspective is rewarding for churchgoers, and can add new dimensions to their interaction with the preaching text. The distance between different perspectives can generate an interspace—or a third room—in which the churchgoers in a critical interaction can create their own new understandings and interpretations of the text as a counter reaction to the preacher's understanding. The creation of new meaning in this way is not dependent upon identification, but rather upon *distance, difference, and otherness*, as Bakhtin states. As in the associative interaction, these things emerge also in the critical interactions taking place in the listener's own thoughts. The preacher serves also in the critical interaction as an interlocutor, facilitating an internal dialogue for the churchgoers.

It is remarkable, however, that a *critical interaction is not identical with a critical impression of the preacher* or an unwillingness to interact with the sermon. The churchgoers could express great appreciation for the pastor and at the same time be critical toward the sermon. What primarily constitutes the churchgoers' sympathy with the preacher is whether the listeners perceive the preacher as authentic, respectful and open towards them—not whether they share the preacher's theology or interpretation of texts. Several churchgoers even expressed that they liked to interact with different perspectives, and it was a part of their motivation to listen to sermons:

> I like to listen to other opinions (in the sermon), which is not in line with mine, since it provides for me the opportunity to reflect.[68]

This is noteworthy, as many pastors express their concern or even fear of offending the congregation; they think that the listeners need to be in line with their perspectives in order to listen to their sermons. The preacher's different interpretation of the text, however, is appreciated since the listeners do not simply absorb the preacher's position, but are encouraged to generate new insights in the wake of the critical interaction. The gospel sometimes offends, and turns our perspective upside down, and challenges our values. The listeners appreciate this provocative voice of the gospel presented in the preacher's sermons, as long as they perceive the preacher to be authentic, open, and respectful.

A representative example of the critical interaction is a 44-year-old man who had his daughter baptized. He created his own inner sermon

---

68. A 91-year-old woman listening to a radio transmitted worship service.

through critical dialogue, by linking the preacher's talk about Hell to an experience in his childhood. He was aware that his interpretation differed from the preacher's, and he elaborated and transformed an illustration in the sermon to suit his own experiences. The preacher said in the sermon (based on Luke 16:19–31, about Lazarus and the rich man), that there is a gap between Heaven and Hell, which makes it impossible to move from one to the other, even though it is possible to look from one side to another. The interviewee, however, explained that in his imagination—while he was listening to the sermon—the gap was filled with water, even though he knew that this was not what the preacher had meant. Yet it was important for him to bridge the gap. He identified Hell as loneliness, with lonely humans seeing humans in community in Heaven. He explained how he as a child had felt isolated and experienced loneliness, standing on one side of a gap that separated him from the people around him. Obviously it was important for him to make his way out of loneliness and become a part of the surrounding community. By means of association he created an analogy based on the fact that it was possible to see from one place to the other, so in his imagination, Jesus filled the gap with water, making it possible bridge the gap. Since he had his daughter baptized, I wondered what the water meant to the listener, and asked him, and he answered "forgiveness." The preacher never mentioned the words loneliness, community, or forgiveness in the sermon, but those were the keywords for the interviewee.

This churchgoer demonstrated some typical features of the critical interaction:

- The interviewee expresses great appreciation for the preacher.
- At the same time the listener is critical toward the sermon.
- The churchgoer is unable to identify or empathize with the preacher's perspective.
- The listener's inner sermon is activated by the preacher's different perspective.
- The listener creates his or her inner sermon through a critical interaction in the search for personal meaning/understanding.
- The churchgoer's inner sermon differs radically from the preacher's sermon.
- The listener is aware of the different semantic meaning between the preacher's expression and the listener's constructed inner sermon.

- But, the inner meaning, counts for the listener.
- The outer words of the sermon crash with inner convictions and create a third new meaning.
- The churchgoer appreciates being challenged in his way of thinking.
- The challenge through the sermon generates new meaning, questions and expands the perspective on life.
- The expanded perspective on life is actually why the listener attends church.

In this way the preacher is a dialogue partner and a facilitator for new insights for the listener, based on the disagreements between them. The preacher's role in recent homiletical literature has been described as the *fool who is interrupting* people. "For preachers proclaim the foolish, disruptive gospel of the life, death, and resurrection of Jesus."[69] This foolish interruption is, however, not to be seen as an accidental destruction, since the interruption contributes to open up a liminal space which is open for interpretation, and "liminality implies an ambiguous phase between two situations or statuses."[70] The empirical findings support the idea that the preacher's different perspectives interrupt the churchgoers' pre-understandings, which can be the case in the critical interaction. Yet it is remarkable, that if the critical interaction is understood as interruption, then the churchgoers in the interviews appreciate this interruption, because most of them valued being challenged by different perspectives. It provides for the listeners an opportunity to reflect, and their reflections either confirmed their pre-understandings, or expand and transform their understandings.

The starting point for the critical dialogue were the listener's *pre-understandings* which they typically related to theological *ideas and conceptions* or to concrete *life experiences*. An interesting finding is that the critical response based upon ideas and conceptions seems less willing to be moved by the encounter with a different perspective, while the critical response based upon life experience seems more willing to be moved in the critical process of reasoning and understanding. However, only few of the interviewees were not moved in one way or another. Following Bakhtin's understanding of the dialogical interaction, the creation of new meaning on the part of the listener "depends on a strong, though flexible

---

69. Campbell and Cilliers, *Preaching Fools*, 153.
70. Campbell and Cilliers, *Preaching Fools*, 41.

relationship between the other and I," which was in general not found in the critical dialogue with regard to the churchgoers' theological ideas and pre-conceptions.

An example is a 74-year-old retired woman, listening to a radio-transmitted service who turned off the radio when the preacher did not speak the Word of God. When I asked her how she could determine whether it was the Word of God, she answered that the Spirit told her; and to the question of how she knows that it is the Spirit talking to her, she answered, that she knows from her Sunday school training as a child. Her critical response was based upon theological conceptions founded in her childhood and she was not willing to be moved in the encounter with a different perspective, so she turned off the radio.[71] The churchgoers who based their critical responses upon ideas and conceptions were likely to have an understanding of the Bible as an external authority, containing an objective truth which they had direct access to. From their point of view, the Bible was an unambiguous text, with which they could identify and empathize, and in that sense, they were in control of their perceptions of the truth.

An example of a 63-year-old churchgoer who also responded critically to the preacher's perspective but related the perspective in a different way to her own life experience:

> I thought, this can't be true, that she (the preacher) knows someone like this […], you project it to your own experiences: Do I know someone who is like this? I don't think so, it can't be true, there is no-one like this.

But the churchgoer ended up being willing to be moved by the preacher's perspective after having processed the words critically, and the criteria for the process was the churchgoer's personal life experience. There seems to be a greater humility and mobility when the frame of reference for the theological claims is life experience bound to time and place. The *persuasive element* of preaching being able to move churchgoers in new directions is *not the Bible as an authority per se*, but the listeners' internal *critical dialogue* with the Bible and the preacher's interpretation of the text. These interactions activate the creation of new meaning and understanding by relating to the listeners' life experiences. Or to put it another way, an

---

71. A correspondingly critical voice could here draw parallel to Martin Luther's concept of the unambiguous text (*Sola Scriptura*), when he, in Worms 1521, stated that all doctrines and dogmata of the church not found in Scripture should be discarded. Schilling, *Martin Luther*, 207.

epistemic abstract knowledge perceived as eternal theological truth only becomes real for the listeners when they connect these things with their life experiences.

The interviewees describe the importance of their interaction with the preacher for their experience of preaching by referring to a discourse that echoes their own life experiences more than the sermon articulated by the preacher. Most of the interviews witness some kind of interaction—critical or associative—moving the churchgoers from their original starting point when they relate the preacher's words to their experiences. Preaching cannot change their experiences—such as the experience of loss, joy, grief, love, or loneliness is still the same—but the sermon can offer an alternative interpretation of the listeners' experiences so they can perceive the experiences in new perspectives. When the listeners hear and recognize an experience described by the preacher from another perspective, it stimulates the process of interpretation and understanding the experience in a new light of the gospel. This new understanding is seldomly identical with the preacher's perspective, as we saw above in the case of the 44-year-old man, who in a critical interaction interpreted his experience of loneliness in his childhood came to a new perspective, and concluded that forgiveness is the way out of loneliness.

The two dialogical interactions, the associative and the critical, facilitating a third meaning or understanding, are the most frequent in the interviews. Yet, there is also a third kind of interaction which grew out of the more profound analysis of the interviews. The clash between the outer words of the sermon and the listeners' inner experiences sometimes seems to have the capacity to generate not only a cognitive understanding but also *a state of being*, which leads to the third category.

Contemplative Interaction

> I'm constantly aware of where I am, but it is as if… I hear the words, and I think I know what has been said, but afterwards… I can't remember anything.[72]

The above quoted man apologized that he could not remember much of the sermon he had just heard. Several of the interviewed churchgoers were not able to remember the sermon, and they apologized, and felt embarrassed, because they thought tho that they ought to get the transfer from

---

72. A 63-year-old man working as a journalist.

the preacher. They subconsciously understood the preaching event in line with the Protestant tradition's emphasis on the outer words: The Bible alone (rather than broader sacred tradition) is the highest authority in matters of faith. When the churchgoers were not able to remember anything of, or only small fragments of, the sermon, they felt ashamed. However, such a clear focus on *the cognitive dimension of preaching is an all-too-reductionist understanding.*

The encounter between the outer words and inner experiences not only generates new semantic meaning, it sometimes also seems to have the capacity to generate a particular form of being which transcends words and thoughts. I describe this state of being as *the contemplative interaction.* Prior to this contemplative interaction the churchgoers typically have had associative or critical thoughts. The word "contemplation" was not used directly by any of the interviewees, but naming this category grew out of my interpretation of the interviewees' emphasis on experiences of non-cognitive modes of transcendence.[73]

The preacher's words stimulate a mental process, an associative or critical dialogue, but this interaction seems to transcend the words to an extent that the churchgoers afterwards are not able explain what they have heard. Typically, they think they have been listening to the sermon, but they cannot recall the content of the sermon or their inner dialogue with the preacher's words after the worship service. It is as if they have been in a different place in their consciousness, a place for which they cannot account. It is remarkably, however, that they can explain their thoughts, both before and after they had been in the contemplative mode. The interviewees describe the experience of being contemplative with words like: dreaming, meditating, transcending, being in another state of consciousness, or just being somewhere else. The most precise description one of the churchgoers gave of this contemplative interaction was that "It is not of this world:"

> Interviewee: If I have to be honest, I'm often dreaming, I'm ... just looking out the window, I hear the words, and sometimes I close my eyes, ... I hear all the words, but I am far away. I'm trying to recall what had been said, but I can't remember it.
> Interviewer: When you close your eyes, where are you then? Can you explain how it is experienced?

---

73. Comparable non-cognitive ways of responding to worship services have been described by ritual theorists with emphasis on physical embodiedness and situatedness. See Bell, *Ritual Theory*; Nielsen, "Ritualization, the Body and the Church."

> Interviewee: It is not of this world [pause]. It is definitely not. I've never really thought about where I was then, but uh… in another consciousness.[74]

The churchgoers are influenced by the preacher's words which stimulate mental activity, and lead to a contemplative state of being, which I interpret as a form of immanent experience of transcendence. In the interviews this meant that the churchgoers could hardly tell what had happened in their minds, as if they have an empty hole in their memories. Yet, they can account for their thoughts before the mind transcends, and often a chain of associative or critical thoughts has been preceding this contemplative mode. Moreover, it is difficult for the churchgoers to describe the contemplative mode of being somewhere else. It is easier for them to explain what happens to them after that moment: being more "peaceful," "relaxed," or "calm" and finding "inner silence." Some of the churchgoers even said that they attend worship service to relax, to find peace, or that they appreciate the silence. From a phenomenological approach, the worship service is not silent. Rather it is full of sounds from the words of the text, readings, hymns, prayers, and the sermon. So I interpret the silence to which the interviewees refer as a break in the inner flow of thoughts, opening up the contemplative state of being. The churchgoers' contemplative state of being is their experience of a peaceful mode of being present. In any case, this contemplative interaction is activated by the words embedded in the worship service. What seemed to happen is a shift from one state of being to another, caused by an interruption of the everyday mode.

The *concept of contemplation* can be traced back to the Desert Fathers in the third century, and has been practiced and defined differently in the monastic tradition.[75] Despite the different interpretations and understandings of the concept of contemplation, the concept has some common features as a mode of perception. It can be described as a state of being transcending words; instead of describing a contemplative person as having a dialogue with God, thinking of God, talking about God, or creating images of God, the contemplative person *dwells in God*. Through prayer and meditation monks and nuns have throughout the centuries in the

---

74. The same 63-year-old man working as a journalist.

75. The Desert Fathers and Desert Mothers were early Christian hermits, ascetics, monks, and nuns who lived mainly in the desert of Egypt beginning around the third century. These desert communities that grew out of the informal gathering of hermits became a model for Christian monasticism. Mursell, *Story of Christian Spirituality*, 204–5, 212, 339; Lawrence, *Medieval Monasticism*, 1–5; Williams, *Silence and Honey Cakes*.

monastic tradition tried to center their minds by *being in the presence of God, quietly, without words or thoughts*. It can best be described as a state of being with no concerns, no worries, no mental activities, but perceiving oneself participating or being united with God. The German theologian, Ingolf Dalferth, operates with the concept of "contemplative thinking," which he describes as a kind of philosophizing. This philosophizing appears to transform the self during contemplation. It does not change the object of philosophizing, but it changes the subject who is contemplative and doing the philosophizing.[76]

The empirical findings indicate that the churchgoers can experience something similar to this contemplative state of being when they participate in the worship service and listen to, and interact with, a sermon. Some of the interviews clearly bore witness to this interaction, and I identify traces of such interaction causing inner peace and silence in many of the interviews. While the churchgoers did not describe this contemplative interaction as an encounter with God or as a dwelling in God, there are many parallels in their descriptions of the experiences of peace and inner silence and between contemplative prayer and meditation within the monastic tradition. The contextual worship situation also seems to be essential for the interviewees' contemplative transformation, together with the fact that the churchgoers themselves have chosen to attend the worship service, as expressed by this interviewee:

> You can be a little sad when you come (to the church). Perhaps something has disappointed you or someone has annoyed you. But as soon as you are here (in the church), and we are together and we sing, then the mood is getting better. You experience this peace, and it is as if you are a different person when it (the worship service) is over.[77]

The contemplative interaction inspired by a sermon emerges from the situatedness in the entire service of worship. The fact that the sermon is embedded in a liturgical service supported by church music, hymns, prayers, rituals, the Eucharist, and surrounded by a congregation attending the same service in a specific church building at a specific time, obviously play a crucial role for contemplative interaction. I named all three kinds of interactions as dialogue, but the word *dialogue* may seem misleading, as contemplation is defined as non-verbal stae of being. The concept, however,

---

76. Dalferth, *Die Wirklichkeit des Möglichen*, 56.
77. A 66-year-old male churchgoer in the state prison church.

is adequate here because the contemplative interaction described by the churchgoers is activated by (Greek: dia) words (Greek: logoV) dialogue.

Like the other internal dialogues this contemplative interaction is not controlled by the preacher's intention: It occurs independently.[78] Hence, the contemplative mode seems to be more dependent on the liturgical and physical room of the service in the church, than the intentions of the preacher, but, still, the churchgoers who experienced the contemplative mode were talking about their impression of the preacher. I interpret this as the churchgoers relying on and trusting their preachers in order to feel safe before giving up control and surrendering to the contemplative interaction.

3.4 THE CHURCHGOERS SITUATED STARTING POINT

> For me it (the sermon) makes sense when he (the preacher) relates to something I can recognize from my life. It becomes present... and I can better relate to it (the sermon) when it is about something happening in my life, rather than just about an ancient text [...] which is not the time I live. [79]

Not surprisingly, the starting point for the churchgoers' internal dialogues are their own life situations, their personal experiences with joy and sorrows and current challenges. Words of the sermon are related to the listeners' own experiences, thoughts, issues and the questions they bring with them into church. As the churchgoers are situated in different contexts with different point of views, they do rarely—if ever—identify with the preacher's interpretation of the text. The importance of the listeners' current life situations cannot be overestimated for their understanding and interpretation of the Biblical text in dialogue with the preacher's interpretation. The sermon can add something external to the churchgoers' starting points, but in order to make sense, the sermon has to be related to the listener's life situations.

---

78. One of the preachers I interviewed explicitly said that he was aware of this contemplative mode and considered it as a good way to receive his sermon. His intention is to allow the churchgoers to go into contemplative interaction. Interestingly, the churchgoers who most clearly expressed having experienced a contemplative state of being did not participate in the worship service held by this preacher; they participated in other services, conducted by other pastors who were not aware of, or at least not talking about, the contemplative mode.

79. A 44-year-old female churchgoer not used to attend the worship service.

Exploring the Third Room in Preaching

It is characteristic for interviews that the listeners are occupied by a specific theme when entering the church. Typically, listeners bring the sermon material into dialogue with just one single theme or a problem in their current life situation. Only one little fragment of the sermon, or maybe a fragment from the rest of the worship service, typically enables this interaction. Thus, the accent is on the situated listener creating meaning in dialogue with what is heard *on the basis of her or his own life*. Consequently, the words of the sermon are not attributed meaning until they are used in relation to the churchgoers' personal experience. The listeners' experiences within a congregation obviously vary widely, and thus, sermon interaction within a single congregation varies. For instance, four interviewees participating in the same worship service expressed four very different understandings caused by different dialogical interactions with the same sermon—and the preacher had a fifth divergent understating of his own words. Obviously, their starting points are situated in four very different life situations which result in four very different inner sermons.

A 77-year-old female churchgoer spoke in an interview in a cheerful tone about her own death and funeral, the hope of resurrection, and the fact she had to say goodbye to her children and grandchildren one day. When I initially asked her why she attended the worship service, she answered that she was considering a move to this church (of which she was not a member) "because of the last party," which referred to her own forthcoming funeral. Her thoughts were circling around her own death, yet she did not express fear, but she was concerned about what was going to happen to her relatives the day she no longer is here. One little fragment, "with friends in light united,"[80] a line in a hymn that was sung right before the sermon, activated an associative interaction tracing her mind back to a dear friend, who had called her the day before the friend died. The friend told the interviewee that she would reserve a table for the interviewee so they could be united in eternity. This single line in a hymn, sung just before the sermon, had inspired this churchgoer to reflect during preaching upon her own death, the resurrection hope, and the belief that she would revisit her beloved ones again. She did not remember much of the actual sermon. Her associative interaction was based on her life situation and concerns about one day leaving this life.

A 63-year-old man talked about the importance of being accepted and loved in the interview. He talked with mushy voice and had wet eyes every

---

80. A Danish hymn written by Grundtvig, "The Blessed New Day."

time he touched upon the theme of "being accepted," which he specifically connected with the Eucharist. When I asked him about what he had experienced in the worship service that day he answered, "A great joy... (long pause) ...of being accepted." He explained, clarifying, that he felt that every time he attends worship service, and this feeling of being accepted is constituting for his understanding of Christianity. Therefore, the feeling of being accepted was the starting point of his dialogical interaction with the sermon, which was very much characterized by the contemplative interaction. He thought he had been listening to the sermon, but afterwards he realized he could not tell what he had heard—but he felt relaxed and having an inner peace.

A 53-year-old female churchgoer's thoughts were centered on theme of being responsible for, and being present in her life. She explained that she normally did not attend worship service, but when she does, it is in search of what really matters for her—and the most important thing for her is to be responsible for life. She worked as a hospice nurse, and she said that the biggest challenge in her job was witnessing dying persons who had not been responsible for their lives. She did not want to lay in her coffin regretting the life she had. So what she heard in the sermon was, that when life is difficult and you are confronting disease and death, then you really feel life intensely. Then she continued to say, that she can recognize this from her work, "It is so important to be responsible for your life," and then she explained that was the reason why she had chosen to be divorced. Her associative interaction with the sermon was based on her experiences from working in a hospice, and her theme was to be responsibile for her life.

A 44-year-old male churchgoer talked several times during the interview about loneliness triggered by a feeling of not being understood. He was, as earlier described, critical towards the preacher's interpretation of the gap between Heaven and Hell, which according to the preacher's perspective could not be bridged. Yet, the churchgoer elaborated the content of the sermon, bridging the gap and thereby granting the sermon a different meaning—and he was aware of that—and his critical interaction led him to the conclusion that by forgiveness loneliness can be overcome. His critical dialogical interaction was based on an important theme from his life—the need to overcome loneliness.

The 38-year-old male preacher himself stressed that he in his preaching had focused on the human vulnerability, which is a life condition we cannot or should escape. For him that was the central message in his preaching.

Accepting vulnerability can be the precondition for both the facing of owns own death, the feeling of being accepted, of taking responsibility for life and overcoming loneliness. These briefly described examples, however, indicate the huge variations of interactions with one sermon within a congregation, and the importance of the churchgoers situated starting point. The four churchgoers' very different preaching interactions and not semantically identical with the preacher's intention can give rise to a critic of the sermon or suggestions for improvements. The different meanings which the churchgoers ascribe to the one and same sermon can be perceived *as noise on the line* that has to be defeated.

The rhetorical critic could suggest, that the preacher's sermon should be more focused, the preacher should argue better, work on the perspective of the sermon in order to speak more clearly. The systematic theological approach could claim that the preacher is not theologically profound enough in argumentation. Followers of the New Homiletic could argue that the preacher should have appealed in a better way to the common experience including illustrations from everyday life with which the congregation could identify with. The teacher with an inductive perspective on preaching might have suggested that the preacher in order to illustrate the message more clearly should have included small anecdotes reflecting the preacher's own journey within the text. The homiletic movement called Other-wise preaching could have suggested that the preacher should have invited the listeners to a collaborative preaching workshop exploring the texts together, so the preacher would have gained insight into the listeners' different life experiences which the preacher then could have included in the sermon.

Of course, this superficial presentation of the different homiletical approaches does not do justice to these theories, and I am not arguing that any of these proposals for improvements are necessarily wrong. All of the suggestions, or just one of them, may have strengthened the communicative dimension of the sermon, but, still, they are not necessarily correct either. For all the different suggestions for improvements tend to assume it is possible for the listener to control the listeners' reception or interaction with the sermon, without regard to personhood, relationships, or situations of listeners.

The understanding of communication assuming that the speaker can control the listeners' reception can be traced back to a theoretical approach in mass communication—a contemporary widespread understanding of communication in Western society—which will perceive the above presented empirical results as noise on the line which has to be eliminated. For instance, in a theory in mass communication is written: "When we communicate, we must get through a series of filters represented both within the sender and the receiver. This can lead to communication-noise."[81] This understanding presupposes that it is possible to transfer a semantically identical message from a sender to a receiver which implies that it is possible for the preacher to penetrate the filters with the message of the sermon (the so-called transfer model).

Yet, there is no empirical evidence for that fact that the listeners just adapt the preacher's point of view or absorb the preacher's message. One of the reasons is that listeners are situated in different life situation and thus, have different starting points. The listeners never fully understand the other's different point of view through empathic identification. Rather they encounter the preacher as a dialogue partner whose different perspective brings a new dimension of understanding into the dialogue for the listeners. The temptation in an approach to communication assuming the transfer model is the *false idea of being in control*, but the interviews with the listeners contradict this idea. The preacher cannot, despite the best intention, eloquence, rhetorical effort, and profound theological knowledge, control the listeners' dialogical interaction with the preacher's external words because the starting point for listeners are their personal life situation.

The most important thing to realize is that the words of the sermon and the entire worship service interact with the churchgoers' lives and experiences (e.g., facing one's own death, being accepted, being responsible for own life, or overcoming loneliness), and meaning emerges—or, to express it in a theological way, the words of the sermon have to incarnate in a concrete life in order to make sense for the individual. The churchgoers' personal situations and their experiences are obviously the material they use to create meaning and understanding in the internal dialogue which the preacher cannot control.

The German theologian and philosopher Ingolf Dalfert's hermeneutical understanding of humans as *situated selves*, interpreting the world around us in order to understand both the world and ourselves, may be helpful to illuminate the empirical results. "From a hermeneutical point of view the basic mode of human becoming is *understanding*," writes Dalferth.[82] There is no human life without understanding, and the way we

81. Thorborg, *Kommunikation*, 188.
82. Dalferth, "Situated Selves," 10. Dalferth is a philosopher of religion and theologian

understand, misunderstand, or do not understand, determines who we are and what we become. Understanding is a mode of human living whose performative mode is interpreting. It is a dialectical movement where we understand by interpreting something as something, and by interpreting we understand. There is no understanding without a self-understanding of the one, who understands. We understand ourselves by interpreting ourselves as someone, and by interpreting ourselves as someone we understand ourselves. Thus, there is no understanding or self-understanding in human life that is not at the same time interpretation, and there is no interpretation or self-interpretation that is not at the same time understanding.[83] Our *understanding is therefore tied to the situated self-interpreting the world and ourselves*. It may sound a bit cryptic, but the essence is, that we cannot simply listen to preaching and understand the sermon without a process of interpretation in relation to ourselves and our situations. This points to the sixth of main categories, the inter-subjective creation of new meaning, which emerged as the last category during the process of analyzing.

3.5 THE INTER-SUBJECTIVE CREATION OF NEW MEANING

This last category cannot be illustrated directly by any one quotation from any of the interviews with the churchgoers as no one straightforwardly expressed a meta-reflection of the way of personal reasoning while listening. Therefore, I will explain this concept by means of an example.

A churchgoer returned several times during the interview to the difficulties of confronting and talking about problems. In the sermon based upon John 16:23–28 ("Prayer Promises") the preacher had focused on vss. 23b–24 where Jesus says: "If ye shall ask anything of the Father, he will give it to you in my name. Hitherto have ye asked nothing in my name: ask, and ye shall receive, that your joy may be made full."[84] The preacher began the sermon with a little folktale about a man being granted three wishes. The first wish he used to annoy his annoying neighbor. At home during dinner, while he was eating potatoes with sausage with his wife, the man told her about the three wishes. His wife expressed discomfort with her husband's use of the first wish. She complained so much that the man, to keep her quiet, wished the sausage be stuck in her mouth. Realizing what he had

---

at Claremont Graduate University, working on the methodological borderlines between analytic philosophy, hermeneutics, and phenomenology.

83. Dalferth, "Situated Selves," 11.

84. John 16:23b–24, American Standard Version (ASV).

done, he had to use the third wish to abandon the two first wishes. The preacher used the story as an analogy to talk about how easily we can harm both others and ourselves, if we could have all our wishes fulfilled, but God knows what we need. Therefore, we do not always get what we ask of God, but God will fulfill our deepest needs.

The interviewee talked about the challenges the interviewee confronted, and talked about problems in the interviewee's life, and liked the sermon very much, saying:

> Sometimes you can ask for something which you afterwards have to correct. [. . .] Often we just put a sausage in the mouth of the other instead confronting and of talking about the problem.[85]

The listener had of course heard more of the sermon, than just the sentence about the man putting the sausage in the mouth of his wife in order to stop her complaining. However, she related most to this little fragment; she dialogued with it because she could relate it to her own life experience. The listener said, "Actually, I have tried it myself." Then she talked about an experience from her job as a secretary for a police officer who had always time to help young girls, but never immigrants. She was frustrated with this practice, but it was very difficult for her to confront her employer and talk about the problem. She said continued, "But finally one day, I took the sausage from my mouth, and talked about the problem."

The situated listener, in dialogue with the preacher's words and based on her personal experience, *created a new meaning*, which is constitutive for her understanding of the sermon. The impact of the sermon was not the preacher's actual words, but *the meaning the listener created* by relating a fragment of the sermon to her own experience. By means of an associative internal dialogue, she created the meaning: It is important to confront and talk about problems. The meaning the listener created is not identical with the preacher's intention: We may pray to God and ask in the name of Jesus for what we need, but we do not always know what we need; God knows and will give us what we need. But the meaning she constructed was the meaning of the sermon for her.

In this way, the listeners are typically touched by only fragments of the sermon, perhaps along mixed with bits and pieces from the entire worship service. In a dialogical reasoning process, the fragments are put together in new ways in order to make sense of the listeners' experiences. Based on the

---

85. A 60-year-old churchgoer working as a secretary.

churchgoers' personal experiences, they generate new meaning in dialogue with the words of the sermon removed from the preacher's semantic understanding and implemented in the churchgoers' universe—often quite distant from the preacher's intention. The words of the sermon can disturb or provoke the churchgoers' preconceptions with the result that new insights and realizations suddenly can emerge and create new meaning. In this way, the listener's inner sermon is *an inter-subjective creation of new meaning*. It is important to stress that it is not a subjective production of meaning, as it is more than just the listener's own thoughts, pre-conceptions and experiences. Rather the process of creating meaning is *inter*-subjective since it is the *inter*-action between on one hand the preacher's outer words and on the other hand the listener's inner experiences, which creates the new meaning.

I was surprised to see how often this new meaning created by the churchgoers—typically without the churchgoer's awareness—reflected Christian thoughts resonating with the gospel, including deep theological insights, which the preacher did not intend or articulate. The listener who took the sausage from her mouth confronting her employer left church with a strengthened courage to be honest. The churchgoer filled the gap between Heaven and Hell with water, left church with the insight that forgiveness is the way to overcome loneliness, which is possible because Jesus has forgiven us. One left church with a peaceful mind dwelling on the feeling of being accepted and loved by God, and yet another left church with God's promise of seeing her beloved ones in eternity.

This empirical result from a Danish context resonates deeply with the North American "Listening to Listeners" project. John McClure writes:

> It was illuminating, and sometimes unnerving, to see what laity are doing with sermon[s], cutting and pasting bits and pieces of language into personal and communal religious narratives […] In large part, the preachers' words were removed from the ground (paradigm, life world, premises) on which the preacher stood and inserted wholesale onto a very different ground, in each case controlled by unique life conditions […] more often than not, listeners were painting the preacher's words and sentences into a very different horizon of meaning altogether.[86]

The creative formation of new meaning in the worship service in the encounter between the outer preaching voice and the listener's internal

---

86. McClure, "What I Now Think."

dialogue is apparently a profound and a widespread phenomenon.[87] The listeners are independent religious and spiritual subjects, interpreting their own lives and experiences in dialogue with the preacher's voice in the light of the gospel. The preacher cannot grant the churchgoers their right to interpret: The listeners instinctively do so independently of the preacher's intention or "permission." Yet, it is empirically evident that the preacher's person is important for the listeners, and cannot be separated from the creation of meaning, because the *relationship* and hence the *participating persons* are crucial for the communication process in which the new meaning emerges.

I was, therefore, looking for a theory in which the relationship and the participating persons are essential for the communication process, and which emphasizes the dialogical way of reasoning (rather than assuming the transfer-model) to illuminate the empirical results. Such a communication theory I found in a social constructionist theory, *Coordinated Management of Meaning*, formulated by Barnett Pearce.[88] In this model, which the founder calls a *practical theory*, communication is a *meaning-making process*. The theory provides understanding of how humans create, coordinate and manage meanings in their process of communication echoing the empirical results. One of Pearce's points is that the relationships in the communication event set the context in which the interpretation of communication takes place. Every message has a content and a relational meaning, thus, the relational meanings provide the context for the content. This theory resonates with the preaching event from the perspective of the pew.

Pearce belongs to a social constructionist paradigm based on the thesis that reality is a social construct, and especially language and the way we talk about the world is constructing the reality, as we see it.[89] The episte-

---

87. E.g., empirical research in South Korea, see Park and Wepener, "Empirical Research on the Experience." Norway School of Theology, Oslo, research leader, Tone Stageland Kaufman, points towards a forthcoming research project, *Mer enn ord*. On the North American project, see McClure et al., *Listening to Listeners*.

88. Barnett Pearce (1943–2011) was a North American professor in psychology who was inspired by pragmatism (John Dewey and William James), social constructionism, and language philosophy (Ludwig Wittgenstein). In the 1970s Pearce together with Vernon E. Cronen developed the communication model, Coordinated Management of Meaning (CMM).

89. Unlike some other social constructionist positions, Pearce do not reject the idea that there is a reality beyond our human consciousness, unknown to us. Yet following the Kantian tradition he maintains that we do not have other access to knowledge about the world than through the filters of our senses and our language. Therefore, a transcendent

mological premise is that the world can only be experienced through the subject perceiving it, and that we humans are always in an interpretation situation of the perceived reality. Our understanding and knowledge of reality are, therefore, partially or entirely a product of our own interpretations. Humans' interpretations and understandings are formed in the relationships in which we participate, and the knowledge we achieve is created in those relationships. Thus, Pearce locates the source of meaning in the relational connection among people.

For Pearce, communication is about the creation of meaning, but not in the sense of just passively receiving a message. Rather, argues Pearce, we live in lives filled with meanings, and one of our life challenges is to manage those meanings so that we can make our social worlds coherent and live within them with honor and respect. This process of managing our meanings, however, is never done in isolation, as we always and necessarily coordinate the way we manage our meanings with other people.[90] Therefore, communication is about the coordinated management of meaning.[91] According to Pearce, the transfer model is problematic, because it defines the goal for communication as the transfer of information from one consciousness to another. This theory assumes that a message can be transferred without distortion, and that it can be interpreted by the receiver, in accordance with the senders' intention. In our culture, we have been convinced that good communication is identical with totally coherence between the message and clear thoughts, even though we have to fight a constant battle with the ambiguity of language.[92] The false basis assumption is, that if we just learn to communicate clearly, the message will also penetrate the filters. If the listeners understand the speaker's intention

---

reality is beyond the contours of human cognition.

90. Pearce and Pearce, "Taking a Communicative Perspective on Dialogue."

91. The theory originates in the North American pragmatism and as such is to be understood as a practice theory, which is formulated on the basis of empirical studies of how people communicate with each other. It is rooted in the pragmatic theory emphasizing of the fact that belief, certainty, knowledge, or truth is the result of an inquiry. Interpretations and realizations can be considered as useful when they work in practice. Philosophy distinguishes three classic truth criteria: correspondence, coherence, and pragmatic usefulness. The criteria of correspondence deals with whether the testimony is consistent with an objective view of the world. The criteria of coherence refer to consistency and internal logic, and the criteria of the pragmatic truth links the truth of a testimony with the practical consequences.

92. Pearce, *Kommunikation*, 40–41.

differently than the speaker him or herself, they adjust language in order to overcome constraints and distortions.

This concept of communication is problematic, according to Pearce, because it is rooted in a paradigm, which perceives individuals as separate from one another, and each with their consciousness with a content of meaning. The individual consciousness is, however, more obscure and less private, than we think.[93] Rather communication is more a way to create a social world than a way to talk about the social world.[94] Thus, Pearce inscribes his theory into a social constructionist communication paradigm, in which language is not representation reality, but creating reality. This understanding of language, however, is not a new concept. Theologically it is at least as old the Priestly account of creation in Genesis in which God creates the world with the divine word, and in a Danish context, it connotes the theology of the famous poet, hymn writer, and theologian, Grundtvig, who wrote, "The word creates what it names."[95] The basic idea is that words do not primarily have a meaning: First and foremost, they have a *use* in a situation. "As tools in a toolbox the meanings of words are indefinite, vague and ambiguous, until the moment they are used in a specific way in a real situation."[96] Language *per se* is ambiguous until the context and the relationhips set the frame for the interpretation, and then words are attributed meaning.

When communication is a meaning-making process in a contextual and relational situation, in which the participants are important for the interpretation of the content, then Pearce's theory contradicts the conventional transfer-receiver model of communication which assumes that meaning can be transferred. According to Pearce it is not possible in a substantial way to understand the other, or to be understood by the other. Nevertheless, "mutual understanding" between speaker and listener is not the only parameter for the successful communication. Pearce argues, rather controversially, that communication can be successful without mutual understanding, since the most important aspect of the communication process is not mutual understanding, but the creation of meaning. Thereby he

---

93. Pearce, *Kommunikation*, 41.

94. Pearce, *Kommunikation*, 39–41.

95. N. F. S. Grundtvig ("ordet skaber, hvad det nævner" ["the word creates what it means"]) in stanza 3 in the hymn," Vidunderligst af alt påjord" ["The Most Wonderful of All the Earth"].

96. Pearce, *Kommunikation*, 109.

rejects one of the most taken for granted axioms in communication theory. More important than understanding is the creation of sufficient meaning in the communication process and being able to coordinate with one another in practice. As an alternative to the traditional concept of "understanding," Pearce introduces the new communication concepts which he names *coordinated management of meaning*.

The concept of coordination in relation to communication may not seem obvious, but it makes sense in relation to the inter-subjective creation of meaning. We live our lives inter-dependent with each other, and we are always interpreting meaning in the flow of communication with each other. Interpretation takes place not in isolation, but in inter-action with others. We live our lives in a web with each other and we need to negotiate and co-ordinate our meanings and interpretations. So, communication is not only about understanding, but is as much about the coordinated management of meaning. Pearce introduces two key terms in the communication process, meaning-making and action-coordinating.[97]

A more conventional concept easier to accept in relation to the common understanding of communication, would have been one person's ability to realize what the other has in mind so their mutual action is based upon exactly the same perception of what is going on.[98] Yet, Pearce builds upon Bakhtin's epistemology and dialogical communication theory, which presupposes distance, diversity and otherness, as the premises for fruitful communication. Thereby, Pearce in line with Bakhtin, rejects the premise that communication in its basic function is to understand the others' thoughts. Even though cognitive and rational understanding is a part of human communication, it is not the essence of communication: Communication is, at heart, inter-action leading to the creation of meaning and hence the coordinated management of meaning. Even though the participants in the communication process do not attribute the same significance to words, and even though they do not create the same meanings in the communication process, humans are able to coordinate their actions—and that is the most important aspect of this discussion, according to Pearce.[99]

The notion of coordinating can be applied to the preaching event and the worship service. The members of the congregation are able to coordinate their actions—e.g., singing, praying, standing, sitting, participating

---

97. Pearce, *Kommunikation*, 78.
98. Pearce, *Kommunikation*, 81.
99. Pearce, *Kommunikation*, 83–85.

in the Eucharist, kneeling (in the Danish folk church the churchgoers are kneeling while they receive bread and cup), listening to the sermon, and creating quite different meanings. Each churchgoer participates in the worship service, and each ascribes different meanings to the words of the sermon and different elements in the liturgy. Still the members of the congregation are able to coordinate their actions. In the doorway to the church, they may give thanks to the preacher for a wonderful sermon while walking away with different meanings

As I have noted, if the preaching event in line with Pearce's communication theory and in accordance with the empirical findings is an inter-subjective creation of new meaning, it challenges some of the most taken-for-granted homiletical/rhetorical axioms. Much homiletical literature assumes that the goal of preaching is primarily to communicate an exegetically and theologically correct truth from Scripture and that the preacher's role is to provide this understanding of the gospel at a semantic and cognitive level to the listeners. It is assumed, that the preacher must proclaim the gospel so the congregation can understand God's promise within the paradoxes of life. The preacher has to make the churchgoers come to an adequate understanding of who God is; what Gods offers and requires of us; or how God operates in this complex world full of suffering. The preacher must give the congregation a comprehension of the good news of the gospel proclaimed in the sermon. It is taken for granted that the preacher like the teacher can use words as a tool in order to create an understanding. But what if that is not the case? What is the preacher's role then? My answer is that the preacher participates in the emerging of a third room of preaching, a subject that I address in the following chapter.

4

Implications of The Third Room for Preaching

THIS CHAPTER FOCUSES ON the consequences of the notion of the Third Room for the preacher and for preaching. Initially, I will be in critical dialogue with homiletical literature in order to illuminate differences between the assumed paradigms in much contemporary homiletical theory and in the empirical results of this study. The interviews support the way in which contemporary homiletics grants ethos an important role (especially regarding the preacher's authentic testimony), but I will critique and offer fresh perspectives on the ways in which much contemporary homiletics reinforces the ownership of the meaning of the sermon by the pulpit.

Instead, I will argue that a surplus of meaning emerges in the Third Room of Preaching created through the listeners' internal dialogue. This meaning was previously not present in either the preacher's intent or in the listener's frame of reference. Subsequently I will show through examples how this surplus of meaning did emerge. I address the question of what is required for the Third Room to emerge, and I shall argue that the preacher is not the carpenter of the Third Room but serves as a tool. This new perspective requires that preachers relinquish ego. I shall address the core question of how the Third Room of Preaching influences the theology of preaching, and especially the search for an adequate communication theology, and, finally, I point toward the theological implications of the Third Room involving participation in Christ.

The Third Room of Preaching

4.1 HOW THE NOTION OF THE THIRD ROOM CONTRASTS WITH PARADIGMS IN CONTEMPORARY HOMILETICS

During the process of analyzing the interview material with both the churchgoers and preachers, it became clear to me that mainstream theology of preaching builds on certain assumptions that are not in line with my empirical findings.[1] Indeed, my empirical research demonstrated that the theological convictions embedded in much homiletical literature and practical experience are in conflict.[2] The results are consistent neither with the traditional Protestant concept of preaching, which ascribes an inherent religious function to the listening process and which distinguishes between the divine and the human agency,[3] nor with much North American homiletics more influenced by a pragmatic approach to preaching which gives guidelines for how the preacher can form religious consciousness in the listening community.

Obviously, it is challenging for a dialectical Word of God theology, including an anthropology perceiving humans as *sinners totally alienated from God* (which is prevalent in many Danish preachers' theology), that the empirical results highlight the importance of the preacher's authentic testimony and spirituality. According to a dialectical theological approach, it is not the preacher who initiates faith, but God, so the preacher's spirituality is not a relevant homiletical issue. Karl Barth argued:

> As ministers we ought to speak of God. We are human, however, and so cannot speak of God. We ought therefore to recognize both our obligation and our inability and by that very recognition give God the glory.[4]

---

1. Part of this argument is published in my article, "How Do We Break Out?"

2. Of course, I could have rejected the way people actually listen to sermons and told them that they were wrong! In the best case, nothing would have changed; in the worst case, such a response could push people away from the church by my disrespect for their experience.

3. As "faith comes from hearing" (Rom 10:17), a Lutheran-Evangelical conviction emphasizes the divine agency in preaching, formulated in Confession Augustana article five: "Through the word, as means bestowed, the Holy Spirit works faith where and when it pleases God."

4. Barth, *Word of God*, 86. Grözinger, "Karl Barth, Das Wort Gottes," 158. ("Wir sollen als Theologen von Gott reden. Wir sind aber Menschen und können als solche nicht von Gott reden. Wir sollen beides, unser sollen und unser Nicht-Können, wissen und eben damit Gott die Ehre geben.")

Implications of The Third Room for Preaching

Thus, preachers ought to both preach and to know our non-ability to preach, and then give God the glory. As written previously, Barth presupposed the transfer model, and suggested that the preacher is in the role as a herald transferring the message—the kerygma. The implicit dialogue to which churchgoers refer when describing their experience of listening to sermons stands in significant contrast with this understanding of communication as a one-way transfer from an active speaker to passive listeners. Barth had no anticipation of the hermeneutical problem and language philosophy that within a quarter of a century would seize the homiletical agenda. Yet, what does it mean to give God the glory? Giving up the idea of being able to transfer our own intentionality to the listeners? Yet, as we shall see, the utterance about giving God the glory may be helpful in the understanding of the empirical findings of the ownership of preaching today.

In contrast to the dialectical theology's disinterest in the listeners' perspective, American pragmatism has left its footprints in the New Homiletic. According to the latter point of view, churchgoers will remember images, stories, and anecdotes, long time after they have forgotten the theological point of the sermon because narratives appeal to human experience. That was one of the punch lines in Fred B. Craddock's approach to preaching that helped usher in the New Homiletic.[5] Some of the scholars in the New Homiletic, building upon the insight of Schleiermacher, were aware that the listeners' religious consciousness is related to their experience, and thus, the New Homiletic refashions the understanding of the preacher's role from that of dialectic theology's herald to that of a witness[6] or to a storyteller.[7] For instance, Craddock argues that analogies from every-day experiences can create identification between the sermon and the listener. By inviting the listener at the same inductive trip, as the preacher has taken in the sermon preparation, the preacher can "permit the listeners that freedom of choice that is essential for the birth and exercise of faith" in order to let them draw their own conclusions.[8] The possible conclusions that the listener can draw, however, are carefully organized by the preacher him or herself. Craddock's perspective is inspired, in part, by the Danish

---

5. Craddock, *As One Without Authority*.
6. Long, *Witness of Preaching*; Florence, *Preaching as Testimony*.
7. Craddock, *Overhearing the Gospel*, 3–45.
8. Craddock, *As One Without Authority*, 57.

theologian and philosopher, Søren Kierkegaard who spoke eloquently of inductive communication strategy "seducing" the listeners into the truth.[9]

On one hand the empirical results of this study support Craddock's prescription for using analogies appealing to *human experience:* churchgoers definitely enjoy listening to stories and use them in creating meaning in their inner dialogues. In the interviews the words of the sermon are not themselves meaningful until the moment they interact with the churchgoers' personal experiences (e.g., of overcoming loneliness, taking responsibility for their own lives, feeling accepted, or facing their own deaths), so indeed, experiences are important for faith. On the other hand the empirical results conflict with Craddock's homiletical ideas, as the analogies to human experience do not necessarily provide identification with the preacher's perspective as the listeners are situated in different places, and therefore they do not necessarily follow the same inductive journey, as the preacher has traveled.

According to the empirical data, the preacher does not have the power to control the way the listeners interact with the sermon and create meaning, therefore, the preacher cannot *"permit* the listeners that freedom" to create meaning. The preacher does not possess the power to permit anyone the freedom to interpret: The listeners have that freedom in advance. Autonomy is not granted by one human being to another. Rather, it is a divine gift. Humans are created as autonomously situated selves in web with other situated selves, all selves interpreting their worlds to create meaning and understanding. Furthermore, Craddock argues, "inductive preaching seeks to persuade,"[10] but the persuasive element of preaching is not bound to the preacher's intention. Something else is at stake in the preaching event emerging in the Third Room.

Thomas G. Long points to a weak point in Craddock's homiletic, when he writes: "It is not at all clear, though, that marching someone else through those steps will generate the same 'Eureka!'"[11] Long seems to be right regarding the criticism of common human experience. As a traveler's guide, the preacher can invite the listener to participate in a journey, but he or she cannot direct the listeners traveling. Our empirical research stresses that churchgoers are situated selves—concerned about different topics—who interpret their lives and what they hear in order to understand both

---

9. Craddock, *Overhearing the Gospel*, 67–86.
10. Craddock, *As One Without Authority*, 79.
11. Long, *Witness of Preaching*, 100.

Implications of The Third Room for Preaching

the sermon and themselves. The guide for their sermonic travel is not the preacher; the landscape the listeners pass through is not identical with what the preacher can see from her or his perspective.

Furthermore, Long argues, "When we create sermon structure, we are forming communication, not merely shaping information."[12] Highlighting the performative dimension of preaching in favor of the informative dimension is absolutely in line with the empirical findings here. But when Long continues, "A sermon is a plan for the experience of listening,"[13] then his homiletic conflicts with the empirical results. The entire idea, that the sermon is a plan for the experience of listening, presupposes that the preacher can plan and control how the churchgoers will interact with the sermon. Once again, let me state that preachers cannot plan how the churchgoers will experience the listening process, as the preachers do not know the listeners' situated starting points or their life experiences, what the listeners are concerned about, what worries them (e.g., overcoming loneliness, being responsible for life, feeling accepted, or facing their own deaths). So planning how listeners will listen to a sermon would demand the impossible, namely that the preacher could have (a kind of a clairvoyant) access to the listeners' inner lives, their internal dialogues and the life experiences they use to create meaning in dialogue with the sermon. Of course, it is advantageous that the preacher knows the congregation, but based on the analysis of the interviews, I argue that there is a vital element of strangeness in the other that remains concealed from the preacher.

The way in which Craddock, Long and other North American homiletics continues to rely upon the preacher's personality or rhetorical ability to engage the listeners in the preaching event is problematic and cannot sufficiently explain a surplus of meaning emerging when listeners process the sermon. Certainly, the preacher as a witness sharing his or her experience of the encounter with Scripture with the congregation is important for the listener, but the witness does not simply transfer his or her understanding to the listeners. The churchgoers create their own meanings in the encounter with the preacher's interpretation of text and the Scripture. The ways the homiletical theory of the witness indirectly tends to let the ownership of the meaning of the sermon remain in the pulpit is problematic. The same is the case for David Buttrick who argues that the preacher like a moviemaker can form the listeners' consciousness by using images in

12. Long, *Witness of Preaching*, 96.
13. Long, *Witness of Preaching*, 96.

moves and structures in preaching.¹⁴ Indeed visualizing instead of verbalizing the theology of the sermon is an ingenious approach to preaching, as images create association in the listeners' consciousnesses (as when the listener takes the sausage from her mouth and tells the truth to her boss), but these association cannot be organized and mastered by the preacher. The ownership of the meaning created in dialogue with preaching does not belong to the pulpit.

A contemporary homiletic formulated by the North American theologian, Charles Campbell and the South African theologian, Johan Cilliers,¹⁵ does not directly address the preacher as having the power to control the listeners' interaction with the sermon. They argue that the congregation perceives the preacher as a comic figure, in the role as a fool, rather than seeing the preacher as a constructive dialogue partner and theological reflector who invites listeners to create meaning. Campbell and Cilliers assume that the preacher, having the role of a fool, can "disturb" the listeners in their pre-understandings. The interviews with the listeners, however, do not indicate that they typically experience preaching as disturbing their pre-understandings. When they do experience the sermon as a disturbance, they welcome this disturbance. In most cases, they appreciate a preaching voice not in line with their own pre-understandings, because it provides an opportunity for them to reflect on their preunderstandings, and to formulate their own understandings in critical dialogue with the preacher's position. The description of the preacher as a fool recognizes the importance of the preacher's personality, but in an authoritative manner in which the preacher refuses to use his or her power. Once again—as in Craddock's inductive homiletics—with the preacher's anti-authoritarian role as a fool requires that the preacher possess the power and authority, which is not the case in my empirical research.

We can see steps moving away from this inclination to see the ownership of the meaning remain in the pulpit and the idea of being able to control and plan the listeners' creation of meaning, in Other-wise preaching and in the emerging school of thought that sees preaching as conversation.

> Other-wise homiletics is homiletics that is, in every aspect, other-inspired and other-directed. It is homiletics that strives to become

---

14. Buttrick, *Homiletic*.
15. Campbell and Cilliers, *Preaching Fools*.

Implications of The Third Room for Preaching

wise about other human beings—to gain wisdom about and from others for preaching.[16]

Therefore, "a space should be cleared within dialogue in which the counter sentences of the other can be voiced and heard."[17] Thus, the others are invited to a round table discussion about Scripture, so the preacher in a-face-to-face encounter with the listeners will have an insight into the others' worlds of experience before entering the pulpit.

Another example is formulated by two North American homileticans Ronald Allen and O. Wesley Allen Jr. who propose a conversational and non-apologetic approach to preaching.[18] They address the importance of authenticity and reciprocity between the many voices participating in preaching which very much reflects my empirical findings, and they presuppose a dialogical epistemology. Allen and Allen suggest that the purpose of the conversational approach to preaching is to contribute to the listeners' making meaning by offering a tentative interpretation and experience of, and response to God's character, purpose, and good news.[19] Thus, Allen and Allen Jr. see the sermon inviting the congregation to make meaning of the gospel, which in many ways is coherent with the empirical research. Yet, the empirical findings led me a dramatic step further. I was surprised to see how the substantial meaning of the sermon was formed for each churchgoers by the encounter of inner experience and outer words.

It is often taken for granted in much homiletical discourse and literature that the preacher's role is to provide an understanding of the gospel at a semantic and cognitive level to the listeners. This emerging surplus of meaning, however, is not necessarily related to a cognitive perception, since it can be experienced as an intensified feeling of being present or as a feeling of inner peace, which was often the case in contemplative dialogue in my research. I argue, therefore, that the New Homiletic, Other-wise preaching do not have a sufficiently developed eye for the surplus of meaning emerging in the Third Room of Preaching which cannot be predicted, planned, or controlled by the preacher. While the conversational approach to preaching moves in the same direction as the Third Room of Preaching, the empirical findings of this study push the idea of conversational preaching a step further. In the following section, I will elaborate and explain this

16. McClure, *Other-wise Preaching*, xi.
17. McClure, *Other-wise Preaching*, 59.
18. Allen and Allen, *Sermon Without End*.
19. Allen and Allen, *Sermon Without End*, 102, 153.

surplus of meaning from the perspective of the pew in critical dialogue with Other-wise preaching.

4.2. THE EMERGENT SURPLUS OF MEANING IN THE THIRD ROOM OF PREACHING

> Well, I do not attend worship services to get information, [...] which I have plenty of in my life. I am going to be touched, or affected, or moved in some way, or at least to be in what, uh ... I experience as presence and open space.[20]

Attending worship services and listening to sermons is not primarily about getting information, but rather, it is primarily about interaction that prompts the listener to construct perception, understanding, or experience a contemplative state of being. Working for years with the listeners' perspective and experience of preaching has shown to me, how unpredictable and impossible it is for the preacher to know the ways the listeners will interact with their words, and which meanings the listeners will create in their internal dialogues with the external words of the sermon. There is something more emerging in the worship situation: There is a surplus of meaning, which is more than the sum of listeners' experiences and the words of the preacher. The logic seems to be $1 + 1 = 3$, which is at the core of emergence theories. In philosophy, systems theory, science and art, the concept of emergence denotes the way complex systems and patterns can arise out of a multiplicity of relatively simple interactions. New features can be formed or occur in a complex system that cannot be explained by the individual's properties. The whole is greater than the sum of the parts. Thus, emergence appears because of a process whereby larger entities, patterns, and regularities arise through interactions among smaller or simpler entities that do not exhibit by themselves, the properties that emerge when they come together. I found, that this emergence theory can illuminate the empirical findings, and help to explain a surplus of meaning emerging in the Third Room of Preaching.

This surplus of meaning emerging in the preaching situation is more than the hermeneutical phenomenological approach presented by the French philosopher Paul Ricœur.[21] The interviewees often point to tranc-

---

20. A 53-year-old female churchgoer working as an assistant professor teaching religion.

21. Ricœur, *Interpretation Theory*.

ing the cognitive level and experiencing a contemplative state of being, for instance, the feeling of inner peace. The concept of a surplus of meaning is closer to the Danish philosopher Dorthe Jørgensen's definition:

> The concept of "immanent transcendence" is, indeed, very meaningful because it refers to a specific experience, and an experience that anyone may have, namely when we feel as if the world suddenly opens up and allows a surplus of meaning, i.e. intensified meaning, to open up.[22]

In the interviews, I often found such traces and signs of experiences of such a surplus of meaning. I became especially aware of this emerging surplus of meaning in critical dialogue with John McClure's homiletical theory, Other-wise preaching. McClure shares the New Homiletic's assumption that experience is fundamental for preaching, but people do not necessarily have the same experience as the neighbor in the pew or the preacher in the pulpit. Therefore, the preacher cannot assume identification with common experience, but has to face the other's radical diversity and otherness. Giving up the idea of common experience eliminates the foundation for the New Homiletic's epistemology. McClure highlights the weak point when he writes:

> The problem lay in the largely inadequate, uncritically examined quality of the experiences to which these homileticians ultimately appealed. In short, appeals to common human experience, like appeals to metanarratives, fail to pay true attention to the real experiences of the many people, with their own partial and contradictory stories/lives. […] I will argue, therefore, that Levinas' idea of *proximity* requires that we get into the lives of people through a specific, local, and embodied interaction, rather than generalizing their experiences towards either humanist or Biblicist rhetorical construct of the hearer in preaching.[23]

The real listeners with different life experiences must be heard, because the experiences are different, and not just something we have. "It is something that must be struggled for and achieved." writes McClure.[24] The Danish theologian, Sven Bjerg, touches upon the same issue, when he distinguishes between immediate and a reflective experience,[25] and states that

22. Jørgensen, "Experience of Immanent Transcendence."
23. McClure, *Other-wise Preaching*, 49.
24. McClure, *Other-wise Preaching*, 54.
25. See notes 15 and 16 in ch. 2.

experiences have to be processed and articulated in order to be reflected experience, otherwise they are just unreflected impressions. The articulation of an impression paves the way for the reflected experience.[26] People can have similar immediate experiences but process them differently. For instance, two persons are surviving a life-threatening cancer—one is grateful for being in life, while the other is bitter and afraid of relapse—so they end up having two different life experiences. Other-wise preaching seems to be aware of these differentiated levels in experiences.

McClure argues that the preacher can benefit from being disturbed by the other's different experiences, understandings and perspectives. "What is required by preachers is a sustained, embodied movement towards the experience of others at every level of homiletics."[27] The preacher, in the role of a host, invites a polyphony of voices to participate in a roundtable conversation about the gospel. In this way the preacher, in a face-to-face encounter with listeners, can listen to the different experiences and incorporate them in the sermon, a process which he calls collaborative preaching. However, as McClure argues, the question is whether it is possible for the preacher to listen to the Other and learn about the experiences of the other, or whether there remains an element of strangeness and otherness, which the preacher can never overcome.

I think a roundtable conversation about the gospel, is a brilliant idea. It will provide the churchgoers an opportunity to have their own internal dialogue with Scripture before the worship service in which they often become more engaged. The round table discussion about Scripture can open the door for a dialogue about faith and personal spirituality, which the churchgoers normally do not share with others. The preacher's perspective on the text can be expanded and altered by the listeners' different perspective, so the concept of roundtable preaching can be rewarding for both the listeners and the preacher.

Yet, in relation to my empirical findings, I find the argumentation problematic for why the preacher ought to implement collaborative preaching.

> It has the potential to allow for the sermonic expression of a variety of very particular struggles against *hegemonic experience* within a social and ecclesial context that recognizes that one's subjectivity is not just individual personal identity, but that all identity is, to

---

26. Bjerg, *Tro og Erfaring*, 42.
27. McClure, *Other-wise Preaching*, 65–66.

some extent, socially constructed. It also ensures that preachers are confronted with some of the actual bodies for those whose experiences are addressed in their sermons.[28]

The problem is McClure's argument that in collaborative preaching the preacher can *avoid* what he calls *hegemonic experience* by identifying the real experiences of the listeners through a face-to-face encounter with them. The entire idea of hegemonic experience is problematic because it presupposes the (false) idea that it should be possible for the preacher's experience to dominion over the listener's experience, thus, that the preacher's experience can be hegemonically life-shaping for the congregation. To operate with the notion of hegemonic experience presupposes that ownership of the production of meaning still belongs to the pulpit, for which there is no evidence in my empirical finding. Even though the preachers put forward personal experiences in their preaching, the listeners will always use their own personal experiences to create meaning in dialogue with the preacher's words (e.g., the churchgoer taking the sausage from her mouth and finding the courage to speak again her boss). The gravity of the production of meaning is located in the situated listeners' personal experiences and interpretation.

Even when the preacher knows the experiences and life stories of the listeners very well (as in collaborative preaching), I argue, that the preacher cannot know, predict, or control the ways the listeners will create meaning.[29] One reason is that the preacher looks at the listener's life and experience and interprets it from the preacher's outside perspective, which is not necessarily identical with the churchgoer's inside perspective. Even if the preacher listens to how the churchgoers interpret their inner experiences, the preacher cannot plan how the churchgoers will interact and create meaning in the preaching situation because the churchgoers themselves do not always know the meaning they will create in dialogue with the sermon before the meaning emerges from their internal dialogues in response to the sermon in the context of worship. Sometimes listeners even are not

---

28. McClure, *Other-wise Preaching*, 62. (my italics).

29. McClure is aware of the autonomy of the listeners' creation. In a paper he writes in relation to his experiences from the Listeners to Listeners project: "The deep and pervasive desire for 'connection,' 'care,' 'authenticity,' and 'presence' as the center of preferred homiletic practice was a striking testimony to the desire for and perception of proxemics. At the same time, we were struck by the agency exercised by sermon listeners." McClure, "What I Now Think." In my view, to this point in time, other-wise preaching has not taken the consequences of this observation seriously enough.

even aware of this surplus of meaning after the worship service. The ownership of the surplus of meaning does not belong to the listeners either. I argue that the ownership does not belong to the preacher nor to the listeners but emerges in a Third Room of Preaching in the worship situation as the inter-subjective creation of meaning.

For instance, a female pastor in a state prison church having many pastoral care conversations with the inmates knew her listeners very well. In her eyes, the inmates' lives had since their childhood been full of betrayals, disappointments, and breakdowns and they have had so many bad experiences with broken relationships to parents, authorities, or other adults, who should have taken care for them. Thus, the pastor expected the inmates to perceive that they had a broken relationship to God, as God for her is representing an authority. She assumed that they could hardly believe in a loving God taking care of them, since they had never experienced anybody taking care of them. Therefore, she preached about the love, care and presence of the hidden God. From her outside perspective, she interpreted the inmates' inner experience, as if God is invisible and not present in their lives, but nothing could be more wrong. The preacher's outside perspective and interpretation of the inmates' inner experiences was not at all identical. God's absence was not an issue for the inmates. In quite a reverse of that expectation; they spoke from the experience of "something greater than" themselves. God's presence was a reality in their lives, which they did not question. "Otherwise I would not have been here," as one of the inmates said. The preacher's intention in her sermon was to repair the assumed broken relationship to God, but the inmates I interviewed were all concerned about how they could become better human beings.

It was remarkable, that despite all good intentions, the preacher could not interpret the inmates' own perspectives on their situations. The perspectives of the pastor and the listeners were situated at different places in life. So even though the pastor invited the listeners to collaborative preaching, and even thought the preacher knew the lives of the listeners very well, and, indeed, had listened to their experiences, their situated perspectives were different. The preacher's interpretation and the listeners' interpretations of their contextual situations and their experiences were not identical. However, this awareness does not mean that the preacher should not try to understand the listeners' situation or not listen to them and to their experiences. Of course, such practices are rewarding for the preaching event—not because the preacher can avoid the transfer of hegemonic experiences, but

Implications of The Third Room for Preaching

because these practices are fruitful for the relationship and the dialogical interaction. They are fruitful not in the sense of transferring from preacher to pew, but in the sense of the sermon bearing fruit through the inner dialogues it feeds.

The preacher can learn from the listeners' different perspectives, and the listeners will experience a preacher with an open and respectful attitude towards the listeners. The preacher can listen, learn and be inspired by the churchgoers, but has to be honest to his or her own perspectives and interpretations in order to be authentic. According to my empirical research, the listeners will always create their own meanings. By giving up the false idea of being able to transfer, one's own perspective to the listeners, the preacher accepts not being able to plan how the churchgoers will interact and create meaning in dialogue with the sermon, and thereby the preacher respects the listeners' different perspective and experiences, and the "otherness" of the listener, which is exactly the goal for Other-wise preaching.[30]

Here is another example for why the preacher cannot plan how churchgoers will interact and create meaning in their sermonic dialogue. This interview highlights how the surplus of meaning emerges in the situation and depends on the entire worship service. When I asked an 80-year-old man, a regular churchgoer and member of the church board for more than 40 years, what he had experienced in the sermon, he answered: "I would like to turn it around." Then he shifted focus from the sermon to his own life, which is a brilliant example of the importance of a churchgoer's situated starting point. He talked for a long time about a journey he had made together with members of a Danish congregation to Argentina two months earlier. After a very detailed description of the journey, he told about a worship service in Argentina, which had made a strong impact upon him. I followed his associative discourse wondering how this travel experience might related to the sermon experience he had just had. When I asked him whether he had been thinking about this journey during the sermon he answered, "Yes, of course, it was such a wonderful experience." But when I asked him about the link between the journey and the sermon, he replied, as if he first then realized that the connection was not obvious:

> Well, I do not know why I suddenly remembered that experience during the sermon; it has nothing to do with the sermon at all.

---

30. McClure, *Other-wise Preaching*, 8–9.

I did not trace the question of the connection further, but continued the interview. At the end of the interview, I asked (as I did in all the interviews) whether the interviewee had something to add before we finished the interview, and he replied:

> What I am saying now, you will probably not believe, but I haven't received Holy Communion since I was confirmed. That was actually something I learned in Argentina, or maybe it was the first time I participated in the Eucharist.

Then he explained that since this worship service in Argentina, he has received Communion every time he had attended worship, and he liked it very much because it gave him a feeling of inner peace; he had a feeling of something religiously was happening without being able to express it in words. He said, that he himself was surprised that he had to be 80 years old and travel the long way from Denmark to Argentina, to learn to participate in Holy Communion.

The meaning of the preaching event to this churchgoer was only to a limited extend determined by a cognitive understanding of the sermon. However, a third room was facilitated in the worship situation with the sacrament by the encounter between the preacher's words and the interviewee's travel experience, which created a surplus of meaning—in this case an unspoken joy and feeling of inner peace by participating in the Eucharist. The topic of the sermon was not at all about the Holy Communion. The preacher did not even mention the word Eucharist or Communion, but I interpret the listener's experience as an emerging surplus of meaning, activated by the presence in the worship service and by listening to the preacher's words. This churchgoer's "inner sermon" is not at all identical with the preacher's intended meaning, but it cannot be ascribed to churchgoers' travel experience alone. It is definitely dependent on the situation and the participants, and at the same time, there is a surplus of meaning, which cannot be explained only by participants or the situation, but it emerges in the encounter in between them.

When I asked the interviewee what he had experienced in the sermon, he told me what the encounter with the sermon in the worship situation had done to him, namely, it sent him on a journey down his memory lane. His starting point was the situated self, interpreting his experiences from Argentina in a contemplative dialogue with the preacher's voice embedded in the worship service. If this churchgoer had participated in collaborative preaching, would the preacher in a face-to-face encounter have gained

Implications of The Third Room for Preaching

insight to this churchgoer's experience, and thereby be able to know or even plan how the listener would hear the sermon and create meaning? Probably not—if for no other reason than that the churchgoer did not know himself why his memory had gone to Argentina during the sermon. He was not even aware of how his experiences interacted with the entire worship service or how the surplus of meaning (his inner feeling of peace) emerged. It just happened.

I argue that the preacher will not necessarily have access to this kind of experiences in collaborative preaching. In relation to the other's (religious) life there seem to be an unpredictable room, to which the preacher does not have access. An element of otherness remains concealed for the preacher—no matter how empathetic listening, open, or attentive to the other the pastor is in collaborative preaching. The Other has its own integrity, which cannot—and I will add shall not—be exceeded. Ronald Allen phrases this precisely when he writes, "We can never completely know any of these trans-human Others fully. We can never completely possess or control them."[31] Nevertheless, the encounter with the Other in collaborative preaching is a brilliant idea, because it:

> can prompt us to recognize the limitations of our perceptions and can encourage us to imagine possibilities that we may not previously have considered for ourselves, Others, and the world.[32]

The otherness and strangeness, however, which cannot or should not be penetrated by the preacher, is a condition for preaching, which allows for the unpredictable surplus of meaning to emerge. The encounter between the listeners' inner experience and the preacher's outer words facilitates what I call *The Third Room of Preaching* in which the listeners in an internal dialogue create a surplus of meaning that was previously not present in either the preacher's intent or the listener's frame of reference. The meaning is not embedded in the preacher's words, nor in the listeners pre-understanding. The ownership of this surplus of meaning does not belong to the preacher or to the listener, but it emerges in the specific worship situation. Homiletical theories, however, formulated by academic trained theologians tend to focus on the cognitive dimension of the preaching event, neglecting that preaching is not only about understanding the gospel and talking about God, but is as much about interacting with the words of the gospel

---

31. Allen, *Preaching and the Other*, 32.
32. Allen, *Preaching and the Other*, 33.

in dialogue with the preacher's interpretation—and even interacting with God. According to my empirical findings, the preaching event can be experienced as creating a surplus of meaning, leaving the listener with inner peace and silence, or an intensified feeling of being present, which I interpret as an immanent experience of transcendence.

4.3 THE PREACHER AS A TOOL, NOT THE CARPENTER, IN CONSTRUCTING THE THIRD ROOM

The obvious question is, of course, should preachers do certain things theologically, homiletically, or rhetorically in order to create the Third Room for the listeners? The rejection of the transfer model does not imply that factual or background information cannot be transferred, for instance, if the preacher explains living conditions in the ancient world or how society was organized in Judea, Samaria, and Galilee. But the meaning each listener ascribes to the specific information, or how they use the information to create meaning, cannot be controlled by the preacher. This could lead to the wrong conclusion, that when the listeners do not understand the sermon in accordance with the preacher's intention, then the preacher does not need to strive for clarity or to communicate as clearly as possible. Nothing could be more wrong!

Preachers do not have the power to control the listeners' interaction with the sermon, but they are still responsible for their participation in the preaching event. Just because the listeners do not absorb the preacher's message in a one-to-one way, it does not mean, that the preachers should not try to express themselves clearly. Exactly the opposite is the case. Preachers who carefully try to express themselves honestly and openly, who show how Scripture elucidates their lives, and how the gospel touches them, are experienced as an authentic voice, facilitating an encounter between the experience and lives of the congregants present in the worship service and the gospel lesson. In the process of expressing oneself clearly and understandably, the preacher can participate in the creation of the Third Room—a liminal space in which new understandings and or a surplus of meaning can emerge.

It could sound like a good idea to have a recipe or a practical list of how to form the sermon rhetorically and theologically. And indeed, there are a lot of rhetorical skills the preacher can learn, well from the New Homiletic, e.g., focus, function, imagination, narrative, argumentation, disposition, moves and structure. Preachers have much to learn from by

Implications of The Third Room for Preaching

roundtable conversation and by listening to the experiences of parishioners. And of course, there are necessary exegetical, historical and theological perspectives presupposed for all preachers—all essential and good tools for a preacher to learn. But in the preaching event the preacher is not using the tools to create the Third Room. The preacher *is* the tool to be used. So there is no quick fix recipe, no "hand-on-how-to-do-list." There are "only" open hands receiving what God offers, and the preacher's faith!

These things may sound cryptic, so let me explain. The paradox is that the preacher is not the carpenter, the builder, of the Third Room, but the Third Room depends upon the preacher's *willingness to serve as the tool* in order to "build" the Third Room. It is a room, that the preacher (or the listener for that matter) cannot create, control or occupy, but a preacher can serve as a tool offering him- or herself in the hand of the "real carpenter" creating the Third Room. Thus, the tool is the servant of the gospel, so to speak.

One of the pastors I interviewed explicitly said, he experienced himself as a servant of the gospel, and he subsequently told how he experiences the worship service:

> According to my experience, there is a special heartbeat or pulse in the worship service […] The very moment the service begins, I *relax* and *participate* in something bigger. It is a process, bigger than me. […] In a way, the worship service is a form for…uh…I *let* what is happening *flow* through me. It may sound very heretical, but it's actually how I experience it, as a flow. [33]

I interpret this pastor's experience as equivalent to the listeners' experience of a surplus of meaning emerging in the third room. The preacher did not talk be about managing, conducting, or leading the worship service, or about being in control when he is preaching, or about forming the listeners' consciousness. The preacher prepares, and then just accepts what happens in the worship service, letting it flow through him. Preachers, like listeners, *participates in something bigger* than themselves. The preparation of the sermon, the service, and the preaching are a *process*, which can be experienced as a *flow*. I see this pastoral experience as corresponding with the churchgoers' experience of preaching in the worship service as an event in which new meaning or a surplus of meaning can emerge. The process depends upon the participants but cannot be organized by them as they "only" participate in something bigger than themselves—as we saw in the

33. A 38-year-old male pastor (my italics).

logic of emergent theories (1+1 = 3). The semantic meaning of the words is not fixed. Rather, meaning emerges in the encounter between the listeners' experiences and the words of the worship service in a flowing process.

It is interesting to look at the verbs the preacher quoted above, uses for the purpose of exploring whether preachers might be able to do certain things to create the Third Room for the listeners. The preacher uses the verbs: "relax," "participate," "let" (something) "flow" (through oneself), and the preacher uses the expression to "serve" (the gospel), too. So in order to create the Third Room, preachers should relax, while participating in something bigger than themselves, and let the process flow through them, serving as a tool for the gospel. Thus, preachers can make themselves available without knowing what is going to happen. They do not have the power to control the process and outcome of the preaching event in the worship service. They can "only" serve as a tool for the real carpenter and creator of the Third Room of Preaching.

The preacher cannot master or occupy the Third Room but is called upon to engage and participate in it. As noted, this perspective does not mean that the preacher should not make an effort to preach. The goal is still to be authentic and to have integrity and preach from personal faith experience, as requested by churchgoers. It does not suspend former rhetorical instructions for clear and exact expression. By investing oneself honestly with respect for the churchgoers' different experiences and pre-understandings, the preacher can participate in creating the event in which the surplus of meaning emerges within the listeners' inner dialogue. This is not done by explaining how the churchgoers are to *understand* God or the gospel. According to my empirical research, the listening process is not primarily about understanding the preacher's intended meaning but is about the emerging of a third room in which new understandings or a surplus of meaning can incarnate in the lives of the listeners. This happens, in part as the preacher him or herself *trusts* that the meaning will emerge!

Thus is my suggestion for, what the preachers can do in addition to acquiring theological knowledge and rhetorical skill: Relinquish the ego in order that preacher and sermon may serve as a tool whose purpose is to contribute to the Third Room. Often preachers struggle so hard to be good preachers that they are afraid to fail; they fear not being theologically profound and rhetorically eloquent enough, not being able to fulfill the expectations of the congregation, and not being accepted for the preaching voice he or she has to offer. The paradox is that this fear reinforces the

Implications of The Third Room for Preaching

ego and gives the preacher the feeling that the sermon is only about the preacher's performance. So, knowing that the preacher him or herself is not the carpenter, but the tool, can remove some of the fear for not being a good voice of the living gospel. The preacher does not create the Third Room, and nor does the listener. The Third room emerges in the interaction by means of the participants' willingness to surrender themselves into the Third room—just as the good jazz musician knowing the musical scale and instrument can surrender him or herself to the music. Preachers must give up the idea of controlling the production of meaning related to the sermon, and instead surrender to the preaching event by "relaxing," "participating in something bigger," "letting what is happening (in the worship service) flow through themselves," in order to "serve" the gospel, as the quoted preacher said. The preacher whom I interviewed, however, thought that this sounds "very heretical." But why should it be heretical when this experience is related to God, as an immanent experience of transcendence?

At the risk of oversimplification, I see two different approaches to preaching in today's homiletical literature (and maybe they reflect two different Christian ways of being in the world) arising from the *two different concepts of God*, which implies two different anthropologies, and two different understandings of the human—divine relationship, and two different assumed communications theories. These two approaches are quite different, and I think that the two conflicting paradigms can be found not only in North American contemporary homiletics, but also in homiletical theories in Europe.

One tends to perceive God as a transcendent reality, an immovable being, which makes everything else move. With this image of God, the preachers work *for* God, spend all their talents and efforts in preaching, talking about God, explaining whom God is, and what God offers and requires from us, to make the congregation come to an adequate understanding of God. In this positivistic position, language is understood as a tool to transport theological truths from the Bible to the listeners. Here the preacher easily is seen as the carpenter and theology is understood as ontology in which the preacher speaks independently of her or his own position and personality. The embedded communication theory is the transfer model.

The other perceives God as an eternal flow pouring Godself out. Everything God creates, happens in this flow. With this concept of God, the preachers work *in* God. Here, the preachers do not work for God, as we humans are the work of God, and therefore we work *in* God. Everything comes from God and everything happens in God.[34] We are small tools in the hand of God, to whom we can make ourselves available. This view resonates with the social constructionist position, which is in line with the empirical reports in this study regarding the experience of the importance of the preacher's person. Here the subjectivity of the preacher is participating in the preaching event, and language creates rather than transports meaning. Theology is more likely to be understood as epistemology, a process in which the preacher is participating as a tool. With this later approach, we can refrain from the temptation to consider ourselves as the carpenters of the Third Room. This view can accommodate the idea that the ownership of the Third Room does not belong to the pulpit: Preachers need to make ourselves available for what God will do through us. "I am the servant of the Lord; may it be to me as you say."[35]

The German reformer, Martin Luther stressed that in the worship service, it is not human beings who are serving God, but God who is serving human beings. So maybe Karl Barth's utterance about giving God the glory makes sense when it comes to the question of the ownership of this surplus of meaning! In this way of thinking, preachers are called to give up the idea of being able to transfer their own intentionality to the listeners and instead to give God the glory.

4.4 THEOLOGICAL IMPLICATIONS OF THE THIRD ROOM OF PREACHING: PARTICIPATION IN CHRIST

Now to the core question of how the Third Room of Preaching influences the theology of preaching and especially the search for an adequate communication theology. To explore the answer and explain it in a comprehensive way would require an entirely new book. In this section, therefore, I will only outline the contours of a theology of preaching which makes sense for me and invite readers to reflect in internal dialogues (associative and/or critical) on theological issues raised, trusting that meanings will emerge!

---

34. This understanding resonates a panentheism approach found in for instance the Danish theologian, Niels Henrik Gregersen's writings, or in the oeuvre of the Swedish Br. Wilfrid Stinissen OCD. *Panentheism,* which means "all-in-God," is from Greek *pan* (πᾶν) "all," *en* (ἐν) "in," and *theos* (Θεος) "God." Unlike *pantheism,* which holds that the divine and the universe are identical, *panentheism* holds that the divine interpenetrates every part of the universe and goes beyond time and space, but it maintains a distinction and the significance between the divine and the non-divine.

35. Luke 1:38 (NRSV).

Implications of The Third Room for Preaching

To summarize the conclusion of the empirical research: The encounter between the listeners' inner experience and the preacher's outer words facilitates, what I call, a Third Room of Preaching in which the listeners, in internal dialogues (associative, critical, contemplative) create a surplus of meaning that was previously not present in either the preacher's intent or the listener's frame of reference. This inter-subjective surplus of meaning, more than the words of the preacher and more than the listeners' experience, emerges in the worship situation of preaching. Thus, the sermonic event offers an opportunity to establish the Third Room in which this creation of a surplus of meaning can emerge. This surplus of meaning is not necessarily a cognitive meaning with a semantic content; it can be experienced as a contemplative state of being facilitated by a dialogical interaction with a preacher's authentic voice. This empirical study calls for the preacher to be authentic. The preacher, however, cannot control the production of meaning but must surrender to the preaching event. Thus, the preacher is not the carpenter of the Third Room, but the Third Room depends upon the preacher's willingness to serve as the tool.

This result challenges some of the most taken-for-granted homiletical/rhetorical axioms, as the empirical understanding of the preaching event breaks down much of the traditional, implicit communication theory of homiletics that assumes the purpose of preaching is a semantic transport of the preacher's understanding of the gospel to the listeners. The empirical homiletic radically rejects the notion that preaching is primarily about the listeners understandings of the preacher's words. It demands a shift in the homiletical paradigm in order to understand and make sense of the empirical results. At the outset of the study, I assumed too reductionist an understanding of the communication process in preaching. The study itself led me into far more complex theological questions. Thus, I was moved during the research process from actual experience sermon in worship services to core systematic theological questions about how we are to understand not only our embedded communication theories, but also the relationship between human and divine agency in preaching, which includes a revised understanding of the gospel, subjectivity, and the image of God.

By redefining the premises of theological thinking in the ideological homiletic, I think it is possible to formulate an adequate communication theology in accordance with empirical experience. The emphasis on the inter-subjectively situated preaching event is consistent with a paradigm assuming that the listeners participate in the construction of the listeners' perceptions of reality. This involves a shift moving focus from ontology to epistemology, from preaching to preacher, from cognitive understanding to creation of meaning, from transference of information to participating in the incarnation of the gospel. The gospel cannot be understood as a substantial and static truth to which people—with theologians having privileged access through the Bible—but as a network of potential meanings, which must continuously be incarnated anew. Thus, the gospel is something dynamic and alive.

In accordance with this understanding, God is not a substantial and transcendent reality about which we can preach, external to ourselves, but a reality in which we human beings are always and already participating. If humans are participating in God then the antithesis of divine and human actions in preaching is false. Preachers are *in* God (as the listeners are), and as such the preachers are tools in the hand of God, to whom we can make ourselves available for the creation of the Third Room. Kierkegaard (the Danish philosopher and theologian) stresses the need for the preacher's authenticity, because the non-authentic preacher perceives herself or himself as the master of Christianity, and the authentic preacher as the servant. This can explain why the preacher's authenticity is so important for the listeners.

Participation in God can be seen as a gift of divine grace, and "in the act of faith the initiative is reversed: God takes over, leading human beings into in/finite time and space, which is God. Finitude is not infinitude, but it is open to it."[36] If the preacher is considered to participate in God then Christ works through the preacher. The access to the transcendent goes through the immanent. So God happens in preaching and can be experienced as a flow or a surplus of meaning emerging in the preaching event of the worship service. When human beings participate in God, they are not only to be understood as autonomous and limited individuals, but also as relational and related beings embedded in in the body of Christ. This can explain the empirical finding that the reciprocal relationship matters for the churchgoers (and the preachers for that sake). This understanding is consistent with process-relational theologians where everything is dynamically interconnected in God, who is the most relational reality of all; and consistent with Scandinavian Creation Theology believing that we all live in networks of deep interdependence; and consistent with the South African notion of Ubuntu, considering humans as living in a web of interdependence with our fellow human beings and with the rest of God's creatures.

36. Hermans, "Epistemological Reflections," 97.

Implications of The Third Room for Preaching

The idea of participation in Christ and humans interconnected is not alien to the gospels and Letters, but pervades Pauline and Johannian theology.[37] The notion of all living creatures' interdependence or interconnectedness can be a gateway to a theological interpretation of why the preacher and relationship with the congregation is so important for the listeners' preaching event.

Homiletically this concept of God implies that the preachers cannot stand outside their own existence and point toward God as completely transcendent. Instead, the preachers must preach from an experience of being or participating in God. The sermon then will be an expression of the preacher's personal encounter with the text. This leads me to the conclusion that preaching is an embodied interactive event situated in time and place in which both preacher and listeners participate, which involves a homiletical displacement not only from preaching to preacher, but also from focus on the words to focus on the spirit. What does this empirical homiletics, this notion of a Third Room of Preaching, mean for the teaching homiletic? That question I address in the following appendix.

---

37. Paul uses the phrase "in Christ" 28 times in his letters, and the Gospel of John 14:20 says, "On that day you will know that I am in My Father, and you are in Me, and I am in you." These instances can be interpreted as human participation in Christ.

Appendix
From Sermon Formation to Preacher Formation[1]

THE PURPOSE OF EDUCATION in theology at universities is to train the students to critically analyze, evaluate, and debate theological thinking and to propose improvements. This is of course the task of any academic discipline and consequently in theological education, the focus is directed towards the theological curriculum and the formal teaching of an epistemic knowledge. However, the empirical research indicates that the preacher's theological knowledge is not the most crucial for the preaching event.

If the preacher's role is merely to offer his or her voice as a dialogue partner for the churchgoers' own sermonic creation of meaning, and if listeners only remember and relate to fragments of the sermon, one could ask: "Why should preachers work on presenting whole, unified sermons?" My answer is, based on the empirical research in this study: Because a whole and unified sermon represents a whole and unified person, and the preacher's person is important for the preaching event. Thus, I suggest that traditional homiletical education in addition to curriculum teaching and traditional feedback on sermon can benefit with a level which moves from *sermon formation* towards *preacher formation*.[2] It requires, however, a *learner-centered*

---

1. In an earlier form this appendix was presented as a paper, "From Sermon Formation to Preacher Formation: Requires a Room Free of Power," in The Practical Theology Group at the Annual Meeting of the American Academy of Religion, in San Antonio, November 2016.

2. This response is part of response to the larger question of how best to educate and train preachers in light of the presence of the Third Room in preaching. I propose a new dimension in pedagogy expanding the idea of the Third Room into the training and forming of preachers by developing a model of homiletical education in which a similar space (to that of the Third Room) is nurtured between the preaching student and the teacher. This room lets the homiletical students create their understandings in dialogue with words from other students, the class leader, and others.

Appendix

approach in the training of preachers to respect both integrity and at the same time to elaborate their personal and spiritual dimension of preaching.

Initially I will briefly explain why, the empirical results presented in this book call for a *learner-centered* approach in addition to the traditional teacher-centered homiletical education in which theological skills, pastoral competences, and the learner's own personality are interwoven. I will suggest teaching methods, which support both the preachers' personal reflection, and include communication theory in which understanding is created in a dialogical interaction, rather than transferred from teacher to preacher. Thus, the homiletical classroom focus not only on the semantic meaning of the words of the sermon, but also upon how the preacher can be a tool in the production of meaning that takes place in the listener in dialog with the sermon. I will show how preachers in Denmark experience homiletics training which includes a learner-centered approach, as expressed in a focus-group interview with the preachers. The homiletic classroom included traditional lecture on homiletic theory, feedback on sermon drafts, and in addition the learner-centered part of the education. I will account only for the theoretical background and the didactic principles of the learner-centered part of the education. I will briefly present one of the different teaching methods used, and show how the preachers experienced responses from their congregations.[3]

Teaching in the learner-centered classroom means facilitating a room of learning where *teacher's control and power are reduced*, allowing the preachers to reflect upon their own practices, without being judged, evaluated, or critiqued—which is often the case in a traditional teacher-centered approach to learning. So here the preachers are not being rated, judged, evaluated or critiqued but have the freedom to reflect upon their own practice. It may sound like a totally feel-good pedagogy in which the students are rubbed the right way, but as I will show, it is experienced as very challenging for the student preachers.

Although I argue here for implementing the *learner*-centered approach, it is important to emphasize that this does not imply any rejection of the *teaching*-centered approach. Of course, the learner-centered approach requires a basic knowledge already acquired, so the training of preachers can benefit from a combination of the two approaches. Instead

---

3. My experience of facilitating this kind of learner-centered training derives from both homiletic courses in Denmark and from a Homiletic Peer Coaching Program at Vanderbilt University in the US: The David G. Buttrick Certificate Program in Homiletic Peer Coaching: https://homileticcoaching.com/.

of getting bored with teacher-centered education, or losing sight of one's own goals, and getting lost in own disastrous interpretation of the Bible in a completely learner-centered classroom, preachers can benefit from well-balanced training strategies implementing both approaches. It is not a question of either-or, but of balancing and developing the two. Here, however, I shall focus only on the learner-centered approach, since the teacher-centered approach is well-known in much traditional pastoral training of pastors.

EMPIRICAL RESEARCH HIGHLIGHTS THE IMPORTANCE FOR THE PASTOR TO BE AUTHENTIC

The result presented in this book together with other international empirical research highlights that the preacher's *person cannot be separated from preaching or ministry*; and *professional development cannot be separated from personal and spiritual growth*. This empirical research from both the perspective of the pew and the pulpit has provided a richer understanding of ministry and preaching.[4] As explained in this book, churchgoers appreciate authentic and committed preachers who stand behind their words, because the listeners do not simply absorb what the preacher says in a one-to-one intellectual way. From the perspective of the pew, the preaching event is not primarily a question of the listeners transferring the preacher's understanding to their own understanding; rather, what happens when listeners hear the sermon is that they *create meaning*—the sermon becomes an "incarnation" of meaning in which both preacher and congregation are stakeholders.

The results of my empirical research support a communication theory belonging to the social constructionist paradigm in which communication is understood as production of meaning, formulated by Barnett Pearce.[5] He claims that communication is not primarily about understanding, but about creating new meaning. For preaching, this theory implies that the sermon is not mainly about understanding, but seeks to prompt a dialogic interaction leading to an inter-subjective production of meaning. The listener's own story in dialogue with the words of the sermon creates

---

4. McClure et al., *Listening to Listeners*; Gaarden, *Den emergente prædiken*; Fylling, *Hellige ord i vanlige liv*.

5. Pearce and Pearce, *Kommunikation og skabelsen*. The communications model is called "Coordinated Management of Meaning" (CMM). It is not a single theory, but rather a collection of ideas that explore how humans interact during communication.

Appendix

a new meaning. Interwoven in the entire worship, the relation between the preacher and listeners creates the context in which the interpretation of the communication takes place. This is why the preacher seems to be so important to the listeners. The encounter between the preacher's outer words and the listener's inner experience brings about what I call the Third Room of Preaching in which the listeners, in internal dialogue, create a surplus of meaning that was previously not present in either the preacher's intent or the listener's frame of reference.

In addition, international empirical research from the perspective of pastors themselves shows that they experience their lives and spirituality as closely interwoven with their ministry, and that as individuals they are important tools in the worship service.[6] To be a pastor is experienced less as holding an office and a salaried job and more as a personal vocation and being a part of one's identity.[7] Ministry is "less about exercising the authority of an office but more about embodying an authentic contextual wisdom gained by daily practice of ministry."[8] To be committed, speaking from the heart, investing oneself and one's own faith in the preaching situation are also essential for the pastors themselves. Preaching is a part of their religious practice, wherein their own spiritual lives are developed.[9] Thus, authenticity and fidelity to one's faith are key concepts in ministry and in the preaching event from the perspective of both the pew and the pulpit.[10]

The logical question is then: What do these empirical results mean for homiletical teaching and training? And can authenticity in the pulpit be trained? I may sound easy to be consistent with one's own inner faith and outer words, but for many preachers it is a life assignment.

Thus, traditional homiletic teaching can benefit from an additional level that moves *from sermon formation towards preacher formation*, in order to develop and train the preacher's authenticity. It requires a learner-centered approach to teaching which involves a learning strategy to ministry where theological skills, pastoral competences, and one's own

---

6. Kaufman, *New Old Spirituality*; Kaufman et al., "Persondimensjonens betydning."
7. Felter, *Hvad vil det sige at være præst?*
8. Scharen and Campbell-Reed, *Learning Pastoral Imagination*.
9. Gaarden, "Den empiriske fordring til homiletikken."
10. The notion of authenticity originates at the turn of the nineteenth century. It emerges hand in hand with the romantic idea that we are all different and have different capacities and potentialities. According to the Canadian philosopher, Charles Taylor, the postmodern society is characterized by the demand for authenticity, because we can no longer refer to an external authority. Taylor, *Modernitetens ubehag*.

personality are interwoven. This cannot be learned in a teacher-centered training only, simply because this theoretical knowledge about the importance of the preacher's commitment, integrity, and personal faith cannot just be transferred from the teacher's mind to the student's preaching practice.[11] Rather the preacher's authenticity has to be developed and practiced in a "safe learning environment" in which the preacher can grow personally and spiritually.

It requires a classroom where the student's personality, integrity and faith are recognized and respected. The basic idea is that the maieutic approach to learning has the power to change and facilitate growth from inside, and only the preachers themselves know how to improve. With an appreciative approach to teaching, the students are free from the judgmental and evaluative eyes of both the teacher and their fellow students. This is not only a teaching strategy and a learning method, but also a fellow human way of acting—which has consequences for the traditional role of both the teacher and fellow-students.

DESCRIPTION OF THE METHOD OF THE REFLECTING TEAM

Particularly I have been inspired by the learner-centered method of The Reflecting Team, initially invented by Tom Andersen.[12] Here I will present one version of The Reflecting Team that consists of groups of 4-5 preachers. Each person brings a video of their own sermon held in their local church. An IPad or an IPhone should suffice—if necessary transferred to a laptop. One preacher in the group is the *focus person*; one is *the interviewer*; the rest of the group, 2-3 persons, are *the reflective team*. Approximately 60 minutes is used for each session. After each session, the persons in the group exchange roles, so everybody has the chance to be the focus person.

---

11. Educational philosophers such as John Dewey (1859–1952) argue that this kind of abstract theoretical learning simply does not work. At its best, it is achieved by "doing" it in practice.

12. Tom Andersen was a Norwegian Professor of Social Psychiatry at the Institute of Community Medicine, University of Tromso, Norway. He is the author of *The Reflecting Team*, and was the initiator of Reflective Processes in therapeutic practices. The original use of the reflecting team has been expanded to other training areas, especially education, supervision, management, and leadership. I have implemented and elaborated the method in homiletics classes, training programs, and collaborative networks for preachers. Based on these teaching experiences in a Danish diocese, I was invited to participate in the teaching faculty in the homiletic coaching course at Vanderbilt University, US.

Appendix

One preacher is *the focus person* and appoints one person in the group she wants to be the interviewer. The preacher shows 7-8 min. of her sermon for the whole group. Based on the actual sermon, the focus person articulates what she thinks works well in her preaching and what she would like to improve. The interviewer's job is to ask questions about the issues the preacher herself highlights—not to comment, judge or give suggestions or advice. The goal is for the focus person to gain clarification by means of the interviewer's questions and active listening. The interview lasts approx. 20 minutes.

The Interviewer provides different types of questions. The task is to probe the preacher's own experience of the sermon. The aim is to provide specific and precise questions from different angles illuminating the issue the preacher wants to improve. The interviewer shall not evaluate or judge the sermon, nor comment on the preacher's statements, but assist the preacher's in delving deeper. A participant/observation methodology is used in formulating the questions to the preacher. There are three levels of the questions: the scoping, the elaborating and the visionary level. Typically, it will be questions like "what", "how" or "which". If the question gives rise to pauses of thinking, the interviewer should not interrupt. The pauses are as important as the questions in accordance with the purpose—the focus person's reflection. It is essential that the preacher's integrity and theology is respected. Eye contact, a nod and appreciative "hmm", can support the focus person's reflections. The Interviewer will be provided with the reflecting team method guideline to help understand appropriate interview techniques.

The reflecting team listens and watches carefully at a distance, but close enough to be able to watch the sermon on video. The team pays close attention to the interaction of the interview. The team is not a part of the interview. The team can write comments or questions, that they would have asked if they were the interviewer. Since they are not a part of the interview, they should not interfere by talking during the interview. One person in the team keeps track of time and signals when the first 20 minutes are up.

After the interview, it is time for the reflecting team to talk. The focus person and the interviewer listen silently to the team's observations (approx. 15 min.) about their experience of both the sermon and the interaction during the interview. The team shares its reflections speculatively, open to multiple possibilities and explanations, allowing the focus person to "select those ideas that fit". Neither the preacher nor sermon is to be analyzed, evaluated, or fixed. The team's job is not to give advice or make suggestions for improvement. If the team has any questions they would have asked the focus person, they just tell each other now, while the preacher and the interviewer are listening carefully.

The preacher/focus person can take notes and before the session ends, she has 5 min. to reflect upon what she has learned. The preacher is free to answer the questions or comment upon issues the reflective team has touched, or simply reflect upon what is heard. At this time, the preacher is free to talk with both the interviewer and the reflective team if she wishes.[13]

THE REFLECTING TEAM APPLIED TO LEARNER-CENTERED TEACHING

The didactic principle of this method allows for a classroom of learning in which power is reduced, by following the clear rules for communication and reflections. Seeing oneself preach in one's own setting, together with colleagues, can be a trans-boundary experience for many preachers. The underlying assumption is that only the preachers themselves know how to improve, and the maieutic approach has the power to change and facilitate growth from inside and out, activated by dialogue with the colleagues and teacher. With this didactic method, the learner-centered approach to teaching is an *appreciative* one, so that the student's theology, integrity, and personality are respected. This is essential for the secure learning atmosphere, in which participants can reflect on and investigate how they can give voice in preaching to their personal faith, theology, and life experiences in order to develop professionally and spiritually. This approach to teaching meets the empirical need for the preacher's authenticity and involves a learning strategy to ministry where theological skills, pastoral competences, and one's own personality are interwoven.

In the systemic understanding which undergirds the reflecting team—as well as many of the new learner-centered methods—the appreciative inquiry is based on an anthropology which sees human beings as possessing the motivation and the necessary resources to grow in relation to their surroundings by means of communication. The intention and willingness to improve is already *within* the student. Change or transformation cannot be applied from the outside, a teacher telling students what is wrong with their sermons. This will soon be perceived as a threat that activates the instinct of

---

13. For a more detailed description of the teaching method in homiletic training, see: Gaarden and Lorensen, "Das Reflektierende Team."

Appendix

self-preservation, and in consequence one's theology, faith, personality, and one's ability to learn is reduced. Rather, change or transformation is a result of an internal process. If students feel secure and experience their integrity being respected, then they can freely let the ideas and thoughts of others interact with and affect their own theology, thoughts and preconceptions. So personal and professional improvement arise from the inside—not from the outside.

The purpose of the method is to provide a classroom of reflection and inspiration for each participant, allowing for new horizons of understanding and cognition by reflecting on one's own preaching practice from diverse perspectives. The basic rules of no analyzing, no evaluation, no judging, no fixing, no saving, no advising, and no setting anyone straight give the student the opportunity to reflect on deep personal and theological issues in their preaching practice without the feeling of being under pressure.

The method of The Reflecting Team can be applied to homiletic education in various forms. I will here describe another version of the reflecting team. In this version the pastors in the focus-group experienced, one person presents a draft for a forthcoming sermon, along with his or her ideas, thoughts, and struggles.[14] The teacher is in the role of an interviewer or coach investigating the preacher's concerns. By means of clarifying questions, the preachers articulate what they want colleagues to reflect on. For instance, a preacher said, "In this text, I never touch upon the issue of the Second Coming of Christ, since I'm not sure what it means to me, and how it affects my life here and now. I don't know how to preach about it in a meaningful way which listeners can relate to. So I would like to hear my colleagues reflect on how it affects their lives."

The task of the teacher is to facilitate the peer conversation about the issue raised by the preacher, while the preacher is just a listener. Afterwards the teacher returns to the preacher, who now has the opportunity to let the ideas or perspectives of the colleagues interact with his or her own thoughts. There is no right or wrong, no fixed answers in this conversation—only an investigation of the preacher's thoughts, and of the issue raised. This learner-centered approach allows for a polyphony of voices from different perspectives and theological traditions to interact. As

---

14. This version is developed to fit the availability of ordained pastors, who meet once a month, but this model is just one out of several possible ways to work with the reflecting team in homiletic.

previously mentioned, the participants experience this teaching as a major freedom to be themselves (resonating the quest for authenticity which the congregation asks for), an enormous liberation from the judgmental eyes of others, and a great relief that fertilizes the learning environment.

Next time the group meets, the students, who previously experienced the peer reflection of their sermon drafts, now preach the sermons. The teacher does not have to push, explain, evaluate, or give feedback—nor do the fellow students. They just relate what the sermon has done to them, the thoughts and associations, mood or emotions it has aroused in them. The teacher's role is to facilitate the students' reflection. Teaching will be the participants' own reflection on their sermon, theology and preaching performance, and learning takes place in the relation and communication with the responses offered by the other students.

This model of The Reflecting Team suits ordained ministers, as it is a situational analysis of preaching from their practice in their own congregations. The pedagogical approach also helps preachers develop integrity and authenticity between their distinct homiletical ideal and practice. New horizons of understanding and cognition can emerge through the act of seeing one's own preaching practice from outside perspectives and by reflecting upon one's practice by means of questions from the curious and respectful teacher and by listening to the colleagues' observations of the interview.

The teacher's job in the learner-centered classroom may sound easy since it is not a matter of possessing huge expert knowledge and transfer it to the students. Yet, it is quite difficult to be a good teacher/facilitator and even tougher for peer students. Some of the pastors in the preaching class also point to the teacher's role in the focus-group interview: "It is a homiletic training which requires enormous leadership; because the teacher must stay focused and constantly keep the group on track." For both the teacher and the fellow students it is challenging to put aside one's own interpretation and evaluation—which is exactly the opposite of what the theologian has been taught at university, so this educational method needs strong leadership because the didactic principles are so unfamiliar to most of the participant pastors.

Appendix

THE EXPERIENCE OF THE LEARNER-CENTERED APPROACH TO EDUCATION

Finally, I will highlight the strengths and challenges of the method. The pastors' experience of a learner-centered approach to teaching presented here is from a preaching classroom in which the didactic principles of The Reflecting Team are implemented. After one year of homiletical training, the participants were interviewed about their experience and benefits of this kind of training.[15] The pastors experience the learner-centered teaching methods as both very demanding, since they have to put themselves at risk, and cannot hide behind "a theologically acquired bulwark," and at the same time very respectful, encouraging, personally and spiritually inspiring. The method is often experienced as less intimidating than if a teacher tells the preacher, what has to be done differently.

A great benefit is that the pastors can work with the method in collaboration with colleagues once the method has been learned. Because reflection on one's preaching practice is a sensitive matter, it requires that the method is learned properly and that the rules are respected. An added bonus is that the method can help students towards understanding working theologies of the colleagues in the group, especially as the complexity behind the preacher's outer appearance is revealed. The experience is that this understanding can be fruitful for a better collaboration in a deanery or between groups of colleagues.

The effectiveness of the method, however, is dependent upon the dynamic of the group and participants. The method is experienced as challenging when preachers are unaccustomed to collaborating with colleagues, and it demands training to be a good fellow-student (and teacher) who is willing to put aside one's own judgments, sermon evaluations and ideas. Some pastors find the highly controlled form of communication restrictive and artificial. Yet this is exactly why the method provides a kind

---

15. As the teacher of the classes, I was not present during the interviews, which were conducted by a homiletic colleague, Pia Nordin Christensen, who had experience from homiletic focus-group interviews. The pastors interviewed were:
- a 45-year-old female with 15 years of experience in ministry;
- a 29-year-old male with 2 years of experience;
- a 44-year-old female with 14 years of experience;
- a 59-year-old female with 18 years of experience;
- a 33-year-old male with 4 years of experience;
- a 43-year-old female with 10 years of experience; and
- a 53-year-old female with 5 years of experience.

of protection to many other students who experience a "great relief" in the learning environment, where power is reduced, thus, the method as advantageous for their professionally and spiritually development. When the preachers were asked about their experience of learner-centered teaching, they spontaneously talked about how they had experienced traditional teacher-centered education in contrast to the learner-centered approach.

> I never got answers to the questions about the impact of my words, I never heard what my sermon did to them, I never heard about the thoughts it activated, I never heard what they took away with them from the sermon—only whether they liked or disliked it.

It is more rewarding to learn about how the sermon affected the listeners rather than the subjective response about how the teacher or fellow-students liked or disliked it. Being given the answers to the "right" content of a sermon, or how to interpret a biblical text may also hinder the learning process: "I walked away with my head bent, thinking about all the things I should have done differently, but didn't." The didactic assumption that theological and homiletic knowledge can be transferred from a teacher's mind to a student's practice may even be experienced as harmful for the development of a personal preaching voice:

> I didn't learn anything, so I did not know how to preach . . . I never participated in preaching groups, simply because I didn't know how to. I would just have felt really bad, because I have internalized the "theological police" telling me I'm wrong.

The experience of having an internalized "theological police" sitting in the pew on Sunday morning in their church telling them what is good or bad, right or wrong theology is not fruitful for their authentic preaching voice. One of the participants talked about how she says things in the sermon, just because the "theological police" should not be able to put a finger on the academic content of her sermon, but:

> It is like a tartar sauce that we just spread over the top (of the sermon) in order to protect ourselves in one way or another; but of course the congregation can feel you are not authentic, and therefore they stop listening and fall out of (the sermon).

Thus, the feeling of being judged, evaluated, or criticized by an internal "theological police" or external theological teacher is not productive for the authentic preaching voice; rather it is creating an artificial preaching voice and insecurity or even fear.

Appendix

In contrast to the homiletic education, the interviewees had previously experienced, the learner-centered approach to teaching are experienced as a "major freedom," "an enormous liberation," and "a great relief" in contrast:

> I experience the teaching method as a major freedom, because (*deep sigh*) . . . at least that is my experience from the Pastoral Institute, where everything you said was analyzed and evaluated and put into theological frames, and often there was a correct answer as to whether the sermon was good or bad, right or wrong.. The only thing I as a preacher have to concentrate on in the learner-centered education is my own faith—not on whether I have done it right or wrong from one or another premise. So it is a great relief.

One of the reasons for the "great relief" is the learning environment in which the preacher is not evaluated, judged or criticized but experiences a teaching strategy that supports the development of the personal preaching voice. The possibility of individual projections is thus eliminated, which in turn offers students "a chance to test themselves," so they dare to be themselves with their uncertainty or confidence, and dare to experiment and learn from their good and bad experiences:

> It has been so rewarding, because the others (preachers) do not project themselves into my sermon. They only had to talk about how they have experienced my sermon—that is why I dare to preach for them!

The interviewed pastors experienced the teaching method as "safe and secure," "respectful and humble," "rewarding," and "appreciated" because their theology, personality, and integrity are respected. The feeling of being respected combined with the task of reflecting on one's *own* preaching practice, faith, and theology creates a very healthy learning environment, which not only develops the individual preacher, but also strengthens collegiality through which the participants "talk about issues they normally feel lonely about." Despite different theologies, backgrounds, and experiences, the pastors in the classroom see and recognize each other as individuals, each with their different challenges and talents. This creates cohesion in the classroom and mutual support for one another, so the interviewees experience the training as "bolstering theological and personal confidence." This is very important, not only for the individual, but for the whole group dynamics, as the teaching method cultivates "a greater tolerance for other perspectives."[16]

> The method is also an exercise in being more tolerant towards other people, because you work from the principle of not evaluating and rating what others provide; and this is useful (not only in the preaching class, but) in ALL contexts of ministry; and indeed in the pastoral care situation—which actually is at stake here in the preaching class and towards each other. This is a very healthy exercise.

Nevertheless, the appreciative approach to teaching has been questioned: Is it not just back-slapping without any professional and theological development? Criticism is often seen as the means to improvement. If students are not offered faultfinding feedback on the theological content, rhetorical form, or performative dimension of their sermons, how should they otherwise develop professionally? It is often assumed in pastoral teaching-centered training that the teacher or somebody else needs to tell the preacher what is wrong in order to progress.

The pastors I interviewed, however, contradict this assumption. They experience the teaching as "very gentle but also challenging." One pastor said she had never experienced a teaching situation so existentially demanding and personally transformative, so she is often exhausted after the preaching class, as she has to digest and process the outcome of the training. Another said he develops theological self-confidence by learning to put himself at risk and by taking as a starting point what for touches him in the text. Another said he intuitively learns what he only knows intellectually, and thereby learns about himself and develops theologically. Preaching has not become easier, but different. However, it is not only the teaching method itself that is challenging; it is also the personal growth and professional development brought about by the teaching method itself. It is "harder, since you have to put yourself at risk" and "reveal yourself." The pastors agree that preaching has become more personally demanding:

---

16. The teaching method has proved to support collegiality also in the homiletic coaching education in the US where the pastors have even more different backgrounds, traditions, theologies, and denominations than participants in the Pastoral Institute and other settings in Denmark. Participants also developed a strong cohesion. I have applied the method in deaneries in Denmark with 25–30 pastors, where the primary focus was to support collegiality, better cooperation, and cohesion—the homiletic outcome was only secondary—and the pastors also experienced the same positive results.

Appendix

> Furthermore, (sermon preparation) has become more existentially demanding. For one thing is to write a theological lecture, I can very easily do that—I've written lots of essays during my study of theology, both long and short, that's no problem. But having to talk about what I believe and about what I think and about what I'm unsure and insecure about, and about what provokes me and things like that, that is to be *exposed*. And to expose myself is simply harder, and therefore more demanding.

The didactic principle, that less is more, is experienced as very demanding. The group agrees that the teaching method is challenging, but also "encouraging, inspiring, and opening new doors within themselves," and that the outcome of the method has made preaching more challenging. "It has not become easier, but more satisfying," and the pastors experience the approach to preaching as "transformative," and "helpful for personal and spiritual development." Some of the pastors consider the effort less as preaching preparation and more as spiritual growth:

> For me, sermon preparation has become more and more like a spiritual digging, where I read the text for next Sunday, and then I think what in this text provokes me, or what does it tell me, or what in it grips me. And, then I wonder all week long—when I have time, 5 minutes here and there—what in this text is challenging and why does it provoke me and what I can say about it? In this way, I learn something about my own theology, and myself. Then on Saturday night, I write it down and on Sunday morning I preach the sermon. So it is not sermon preparation, it has become a spiritual excavation, about which I happen to preach.

In general, the preaching class participants experience professional development interwoven with their personal and spiritual growth as one of the outcomes of the learner-centered approach to teaching.

The pastors also talked about their experience of the congregation's reaction to their professional and personal development. As a consequence of this learner-centered education, the pastors preach "more personal and less abstract;" they are more "passionate, present, and engaged." They are more likely to "relate to their life experience," and reflect more over "daily life instead of searching for sermon application in classical literature." The participants "preach more by heart and less by manuscript," because they can remember the sermon, as they use their own stories. They put themselves on the line in a way they have not done previously. One said, "I preach for a longer time with fewer words, but more thoughtfully because

I'm now in contact with the listeners." Another said he sees himself in "the role of a co-actor in the listeners' theater, rather than being the main character interpreting the truth for them." In general, the pastors experience themselves as more self-confident and self-reliant and their congregation as more responsive to their preaching improvements:

> The congregation of course has also noticed the change, and they say: "Something has happened. You preach in a different way," and then they like it . . . They say that they can feel I'm more present in the church, because they think that I have a greater confidence in what I'm doing, even though I'm nervous before I'm going to preach.

One pastor said that "more people comment positively on the sermon" and another added that it is more common "that non-regular churchgoers—such as guests at a child's baptism—comment positively on the sermon." There was general agreement among the interviewed pastors that the congregation also enjoys the benefits of learner-centered training. The implications of this "empirical turn" and of the listeners' request for an authentic preaching voice, can be pursued in a shift from teacher-centered to student-centered education mirrored in a shift from sermon formation towards preacher formation—an advantage not only for the preachers themselves, but also for their congregations.

THE TURN TO LEARNER-CENTERED EDUCATION

The debate on teacher-centered versus student-centered education has been in the forefront of learning theories for the past 35-40 years, and the tendency is for education to move toward the student-centered approach. In the traditional teacher-centered classroom, the aim for the teachers is to transfer their knowledge to the students, whereas the focus in learner-centered classrooms is on the student's motivation and ability to obtain knowledge and put it into practice. The learning theories emphasize that knowledge cannot just be transferred from one consciousness to another; for the process of learning is far more complex. Rather the student's cognition emerges as a dialogical response related to other people and in a situational context. Situated learning, for instance, is a theory about how individuals acquire professional skills, extending research on apprenticeship into how participation leads to membership in a community of practice.[17]

---

17. Situated learning was first proposed by Jean Lave and Etienne Wenger as a model

Appendix

So, in terms of teaching methods, epistemology (how we learn) plays an increasingly important role in causing the shift in teaching strategies towards learner-centered training. Thinking, reflecting, acting, and learning work together in a close and dynamic interaction, and none of these functions can be separated from the others. This has led to the redefinition of teaching as the facilitation of student learning, including a redefinition of education objectives in terms of learning outcomes rather than of teaching inputs. One of the basic ideas in the learner-centered approach is that learning happens in the social situation in which it occurs.

Focus in the learner-centered approach is on the person who is learning—not the teacher who is teaching. The teacher's goal is not to provide answers for the students; rather the students ask questions and struggle to find the answers themselves. The basic assumption is that the creative act of learning does not grow out of nothing. The student uncovers, selects, and synthesizes already existing facts, ideas, and skills.[18] The interest in recent learning theories has centered on the importance of embodied, situated, and relational aspects of learning which are reflected in the focus on apprenticeship and learning through participation, and on personal development through reflective practice.[19] Learning takes place in the tension field between cognition (academic knowledge), psychodynamics (personal engagement), and relationship (in the interaction among participants) in the situation.[20]

For preachers' training, the learner-centered approach means that the task of the teacher is not primarily to posses theological knowledge that must be transferred to the student. The teacher is less an academic lecturer and more a leader or a guide who facilitates a room of learning in which the student works in the interplay among theology and homiletic theory (cognition), personal faith and commitment (psychodynamics), and the interaction in a peer group of colleagues/students (relationship), practicing preaching in the classroom (an apprenticeship situation).[21] By giving up control, the teacher and the peer can facilitate a learning room in which power is reduced, and in which colleagues serve as tools for the preachers'

---

of learning in a community of practice, see Lave and Wenger, *Situated Learning*; Wegner, *Praksisfællesskaber*.

18. Andersen, "Reflecting Team."
19. Andersen, *Reflekterende processer*; Schön, *Den reflekterende praktiker*.
20. Illaeris, *Læring*.
21. Illaeris, *Tekster om læring*.

cognition and spiritual formation. The idea embraces the understanding that we learn and grow in dialogue, which is not a matter of one person convincing another.

The French philosopher, Michel Foucault addresses the relationship between power and knowledge, and defines power, not as something one can posses, but as something emerging in the relationship.[22]

Power is present in all relationships as a product of a series of extremely complex and differentiated facts and circumstances, and often we operate within relationships in which the power balance is uneven, and such power imbalances affect communication, cognition and the learning environment.[23] The power imbalances can reduce the learning capacity and create unnecessary insecurity and anxiety. By creating a classroom governed by a set of rules, the power imbalances can be reduced. Preachers often experience the set of rules of no analyzing, no evaluation, no judging, no fixing or no advising as both weird and awkward, especially at the beginning of the process, because the students are so familiar with the interpreting and judgmental way of thinking and communicating. However, by establishing a room "where power is reduced" (of course, it is not possible to eliminate power completely, but as far as possible) the preacher can reflect upon their preaching practice, theology, and personal faith in a conducive way, advantageous for embodying an authentic practice of ministry.

POSTSCRIPT

I have a confession: One of the reasons why I have done this empirical research and written this book is my own craving for control, and my (false) idea of being able to manage how people receive my words. As I argue, learning takes place in practice, in a relational and situational context. Indeed, in thinking about my own history as a learner, I recognize that process was at the heart of my own best learning. If not before, then now, I am absolutely convinced that God is an excellent teacher through these processes (and that God has a sense of humor!)

---

22. Michel Foucault (1926–1984) addresses in his work the different ways in which society has expressed the use of power to "objectivize subjects," and how power can be used as a form of social control within a group in a normal communication situation. Foucault, *Subject and Power*. Cf. "Michael Foucault," https://en.wikipedia.org/wiki/Michel_Foucault#cite_note-Foucault1982-168.

23. Heede, *Det tomme menneske*.

Appendix

As good doctors have to taste their own medicine, I also had to swallow a bitter pill halfway through my research. I was contacted by a journalist who had heard about my project—an empirical research exploring how churchgoers listen to sermons. He wanted me to confirm that the churchgoers' experiences of the worship service are dependent on their experiences of the preacher. I explained that the churchgoers I had interviewed talked about their experience of the preacher when they were asked to respond to their experience of the sermon and the worship service. The following day I found myself quoted under a headline saying, "Preachers scare the congregation away."

Indignant, I wrote to the journalist who, in my opinion, had abused my words to scaffold his own media story. The journalist was completely baffled. He had mis-combined two different pieces of information: People in a diocese in Denmark do not attend worship services, and the experience of the worship service is based upon the experience of the preacher, thus, he assumed it obviously is the preacher's fault, when people do not come to church. His pre-understanding of my words was based on his own (media) story about few people attending worship in one of the dioceses in The Danish Church. My words were exported from one semantic horizon of understanding and imported to another, and the result was a new production of meaning. The journalist was telling his own story about guilt—always good media stuff—and he used my words as a scaffold for his own story. The gravity of meaning making was situated in the journalist's context: his article in a newspaper about few people attending worship services Sunday morning. In the following discussion, I totally failed to transmit the meaning of my words and the intention of my research project to the journalist or to change his pre-understanding.

My frustration despite, the grotesque discussion with the journalist, confirms the results of my research. The journalist's interaction with my words was parallel to the empirical findings: The message cannot be transferred from a sender to a receiver. Communication is not mainly about understanding, but concerns a dialogic interaction leading to an intersubjective production of meaning. The listener's own situation and pre-understanding in dialogue with the external words of others form the basis for a new meaning emerging in the situation. Interwoven in the entire situation, the relation between the speaker/writer and listener/reader creates the context in which the interpretation of the communication takes place.

So, with a bit of luck, I have now learned from practice, and from my empirical research in dialogue with the theory. Even though I made the effort in this book to express myself as clearly as possible, I cannot control the way in which the reader will create meaning in dialogue with my words. I hope, however, that, meaning will emerge in accordance with the will of God.

Bibliography

Allchin, A.M. *N.F.S. Grundtvig. An Introduction to his Life and Work*. Aarhus: Aarhus University Press, 2015.
Allen, Ronald J. *Hearing the Sermon: Relationship, Content, Feeling*. St. Louis: Chalice, 2004.
———. *Preaching and the Other. Studies of Postmodern Insights*. St. Louis, Chalice, 2009.
———, ed. *Patterns of Preaching: A Sermon Sampler*. St. Louis: Chalice 1998.
Allen, Ronald J., and Mary Alice Mulligan. "Listening to Listeners: The Board Reflects Critically on the Study." *Encounter* 68 (2007) 69–84.
Allen, Ronald J., and O. Wesley Allen Jr. *The Sermon Without End. A Conversational Approach to Preaching*. Nashville: Abingdon, 2015.
Almer, Hans. *Variationer av predikouppfattningar i Svenska kyrkan. En fenomenografisk undersökning om predikanter och åhörare* [Variations in Understanding Sermons in the Swedish Church. A Phenomenological Investigation into Preachers and Listeners]. Lund: Arcis, 1999.
Andersen, Leif. *Teksten og tiden* [Text and Time]. Fredericia: Forlagsgruppen Lohse, 2006.
Andersen, Lisbeth Smedegaard. *Ordet der høres* [The Word that is Heard]. Frederiksberg: Forlaget Anis, 1996.
Andersen, Tom. *The Reflecting Team: Dialogues and Dialogues about Dialogues*. New York: W. W. Norton, 1991.
———. *Reflekterende processer—samtaler og samtaler om samtalerne* [Reflective Processes and Conversations about Conversations]. Copenhagen: Dansk Psykologisk, 2005
Andersen, Tom, et al. "Listeners as Authors in Preaching—Empirical and Theoretical Perspectives," in *Homiletic* 28 (2013) 28–45.
———. "The Reflecting Team: Dialogue and Meta-Dialogue in Clinical Work." *Family Process* 26 (1987) 417–28. http://www.willhall.net/files/OpenDialogueReflectingTeamAndersenFamilyProcess1986.pdf.
Aristotle. *Art of Rhetoric*. Loeb Classical Library. Translated by J. H. Freese. Cambridge: Harvard University Press, 1926.
Asmussen, Jan. *Ord virker* [Words Work]. Frederiksberg: Forlaget Anis, 2010.
Bakhtin, Mikhail M. *Problems of Dostoevsky's Poetics*. Translated by Caryl Emerson. Minneapolis: University of Minnesota Press, 1984.
———. *Speech Genres and Other Late Essays*. Edited by Michael Emerson and Karyl Holquist. Austin: University of Texas Press, 1986.
Barth, Karl. *Homiletics*. Translated by G. W. Bromiley and D. E. Daniels. Louisville: Westminster John Knox, 1991.

Appendix

———. "Nein. Antwort an Emil Brunner" [No. Answer to Emil Brunner]. In *Theologische Existenz heute*, edited by John Baillie, 65–128. Repr. München: Chr. Kaiser, 1934.

———. *The Word of God and the Word of Man*. Translated by Douglas Horton. London, Hodder and Stoughton, 1928.

Bell, Catherine. *Ritual Theory, Ritual Practice*. Oxford: Oxford University Press, 1992.

Bellinger, Karla J. *Connecting Pulpit and Pew. Breaking Open the Conversation about Catholic Preaching*. Collegeville, MN: Liturgical, 2014.

Bjerager, Erik. *Det ender godt. Johannes Møllehave om døden* [It will End Well. Johannes Møllehave about Death]. Copenhagen: Kristeligt Dagblads, 2009.

Bjerg, Sven. *Tro og Erfaring* [Faith and Experience]. Frederiksberg: Forlaget Anis, 2006.

Bonhoeffer, Dietrich. *Min tide er I dine hænder. Vennebreve og teologiske reflektoner 1943-44* [My Time is in Your Hands. Letters to Friends and Theological Reflections 1943-44]. Frederiksberg: Forlaget Aros, 2006.

Brinkman, Sven, and Lene Tanggaard. *Kvalitative metoder* [Quality Methods]. Copenhagen: Hans Reitzels 2010.

Brooks, Phillips. *Lectures on Preaching*. New York: E. P. Dutton, 1891.

Buch-Hansen, Gitte, and Frederik Poulsen. *Biblen i gudstjenesten* [The Bible in Worship]. Copenhagen: Det Teologiske Fakultet, Copenhagens Universitet, 2015.

Buttrick, David G. "Certificate Program in Homiletic Peer Coaching." https://homileticcoaching.com/.

———. *Homiletic: Moves and Structures*. Philadelphia: Fortress, 1987.

Campbell, Charles, and Johan Cilliers. *Preaching Fools. The Gospel as a Rhetoric of Folly*. Waco, TX: Baylor University Press, 2012.

Carrell, Lori J. *The Great American Church Survey*. Wheaton, IL: Mainstay Church Resources, 1999.

Charmaz, Kathy. *Constructing Grounded Theory*. Thousand Oaks, CA: Sage, 2014.

Christensen, Pia Nordin. "Collaborative Preaching: A Conversation which Opens both the Text and the Participants." Unpublished paper, Societas Homileticas, Stellenbosch University, 2016.

Cilliers, Johan H. "In Search of Meaning between Ubuntu and Into: Perspectives on Preaching in Post-apartheid South Africa." *Preaching. Does it make a Difference?* edited by Mogens Lindhardt and Henning Thomsen. Frederiksberg: Aros, 2010. http://academic.sun.ac.za/tsv/Profiles/Profile_documents/Johan_Cilliers_IN_SEARCH_OF_MEANING_BETWEEN_UBUNTU_AND_INTO.pdf.

Craddock, Fred B. *As One Without Authority*. St. Louis: Chalice 2001.

———. *Craddock on the Craft of Preaching*. Edited by Lee Sparks and Katharyn Hayes Sparks. St. Louis: Chalice, 2011.

———. *Overhearing the Gospel*. St. Louis: Chalice, 2001.

Daiber, K. F., et al. *Predigern und Hörern* [Preacher and Hearer]. 3 vols. München: Chr. Kaiser, 1991.

Dalferth, Ingolf U. *Die Wirklichkeit des Möglichen*. [The Reality of Possibility]. Tübingen, Mohr Siebeck, 2003.

———. "Situated Selves in Webs of Interlocution: What Can We Learn from Grammar?" Unpublished lecture, Copenhagen University, 2012.

Dean, William. "Empirical Theology: A Revisable Tradition." 1990. https://www.religion-online.org/article/empirical-theology-a-revisable-tradition/.

Denzin, N. K., and Y. S. Lincoln. *Collecting and Interpreting Qualitative Materials*. Thousand Oaks, CA: Sage, 1998.

Bibliography

Eslinger, Richard L. *The Web of Preaching. New Options in Homiletic Method.* Nashville: Abingdon, 2002.

Eriksson, Anne-Louise, et al., eds. *Exploring a Heritage. Evangelical Lutheran Churches in the North.* Church of Sweden Research Series 5. Eugene, OR: Pickwick, 2012.

Fagermoen, Tron. "Ecclesiology and Ethics—Contextuality and Normativity: Reflections from a Nordic Lutheran Perspective." Unpublished paper presented at the symposium Ecclesiology and Ethnography, Uppsala, Sweden, April 2016.

Felter, Kirsten Donskov. *Hvad vil det sige at være præst? En kvalitativ undersøgelse af danske folkekirkepræsters syn på embede og arbejde* [What Does It Mean to be a Pastor? A Qualitative Study of Pastors of the Danish National Church: Their View of Ministry and Work]. Århus: Folkekirkens Uddannelses-og Videnscenter, 2016.

Fish, Stanley, et al. *Mark and Method: New Approaches in Biblical Studies.* Minneapolis: Fortress, 1992.

Florence, Anna Carter. *Preaching as Testimony.* Louisville: Westminster John Knox, 2007.

Flyvbjerg, Bent. *Kvalitative Metoder* [Qualitative Methods]. Copenhagen: Hans Reitzels, 2010.

Foucault, Michel. *The Subject and Power.* Chicago: University of Chicago Press, 1982).

Fylling, Hilde. *Hellige ord i vanlige liv: En studie av kirkegjengeres vurderinger av prekener.* [Sacred Words in Ordinary Lives; A Study of Church People's Assessment of Sermons]. Tromsø: Kirkelig Utdanningssenter i Nord, 2015.

Gaarden, Marianne. *Den emergente prædiken: En kvalitativ undersøgelse af mødet mellem prædikantens ord og den situerede kirkegænger i gudstjenesten* [The Emerging Sermon. A Qualitative Research into the Words of the Preacher and the Situated Listener in Worship]. PhD diss., Aarhaus Universisty, 2014.

———. "Den empiriske fordring til homiletikken" [The Empirical Claim to Homiletics]. *Tidsskrift for Praktisk Teologi* 30 (2013) 3–20.

———. "How Do We get out of 'the Paradigmatic Box'?" In *What Really Matters: A Nordic Perspective on Ecclesiology and Ethnography*, edited by Jonas Ideström and Tone Stangeland Kaufman, 124–37. Eugene, OR: Pickwick, 2017.

———. *Prædikenen som det tredje rum* [Sermon as Third Room]. Frederiksberg: Forlaget Anis, 2015.

Gaarden, Marianne, and Marlene Ringgard Lorensen. "Das Reflektierende Team: Im dritten Raum furs Predigen lernen." In *Predigen lehren. Methodes für homiletische Aus- und Weiterbildung*, 269–75. Leipzig: Evangelische Verlagsanstalt, 2015.

———. "Listeners as Authors in Preaching—Empirical and Theoretical Perspectives." *Homiletic* 38 (2013) 28–45.

Ganzevoort, R. Ruard. "Van der Ven's Empirical/Practical Theology and the Theological Encyclopedia." In *Hermeneutics and Empirical Research in Practical Theology: The Contribution of Empirical Theology by Johannes A. van der Ven*, edited by Chris Hermans and Mary Moore, 53–74. Leiden: Brill, 2004.

Gergen, Kenneth. *Realities and Relationships: Soundings in Social Constructionism.* Cambridge: Harvard University Press, 1994.

Glaser, Barney G. *Doing Grounded Theory: Issues and Discussions and Theoretical Sensitivity: Advances in the Methodology of Grounded Theory.* Mill Valley, CA: Sociology, 1979.

Glaser, Barney G., and Anselm Strauss. *The Discovery of Grounded Theory: Strategies for Qualitative Research.* Chicago: Aldine Transaction, 1967.

Appendix

Grandthyll, G. *Die Wirkung der Predigt* [The Effect of Preaching]. PhD diss., Münster University, 1977.

Gregersen, Niels Henrik. *Human Comes First: The Christian Theology of N.F.S. Grundtvig.* Aarhus: Aarhus University Press, 2018.

Gregersen, Niels Henrik, et al., eds. *Reformation Theology for a Post-Secular Age: Løgstrup, Prenter, Wiengren, and the Future of Scandinavian Creation Theology.* Göttingen, Vandenhoech & Ruprecht, 2017.

Grözinger, Albrecht. "Karl Barth, Das Wort Gottes als Aufgabe der Theologie" [Karl Barth, the Word of God as the Task of Theology]. *Praktische Theologie* 47 (2012) 1–38.

Grundtvig, N. F. S. "The Blessed New Day." In *Den danske salmebog*, 402. Copenhagen: Det Kgl. Vajsenhus, 2003.

——— "Vidunderligst af alt på jord" [The Most Wonderful of All the Earth]. In *Den danske salmebog*, 319. Copenhagen: Det Kgl. Vajsenhus, 2003.

Gutek, Gerald. *Philosophical, Ideological, and Theoretical Perspectives on Education.* New York: Pearson, 2013.

Heede, Dag. *Det tomme menneske—introduktion til Michel Foucault* [The Empty Person: Introduction to Michael Foucalt]. Copenhagen: Museum Tusculanum, 2003.

Hermans, Chris A. M. "Epistemological Reflections on the Connection between Ideas and Data in Empirical Research into Religion." In *Empirical Theology in Texts and Tables: Qualitative, Quantitative and Comparative Perspectives,* edited by Leslie Francis and Jeff Astley, 73–99. Boston: Brill Academy, 2009.

Hogan, Lucy Lind. "Rethinking Persuasion: Developing an Incarnational Theology of Preaching." *Homiletic* 24 (1999) 1–12.

Hognestad, Helge. *Ordet i ordene Bibeltolkning og preken i Karl Barths dialektiske Gudsord-teologi* [The Word in the Words. Bible Interpretation and Preaching in Karl Barth's Word of God Theology]. Trondheim: Tapir, 1986.

Illaeris, Knud. *Læring—aktuel læringsteori i spændingsfeltet mellem Piaget, Freud og Marx* [Learning: Current Learning Theory in the Field of Tension between Piaget, Freud, and Marx]. Frederiksberg: Roskilde Universitetsforlag, 1999.

———, ed. *Tekster om læring* [Texts on Learning]. Copenhagen: Roskilde Universitets Forlag, 2000.

Jacobsen, Bo, et al. *Kvalitative metoder* [Qualitative Methods]. Copenhagen: Hans Reitzels Forlag, 2010.

Jørgensen, Dorthe. "The Experience of Immanent Transcendence." *Transfiguration: Nordic Journal of Religion and the Arts* 2010–2011 (2011) 35–52.

———. *Transfiguration.* Copenhagen: Museum Tusculanum, 2010.

Kaufman, Tone Stangeland. "From the Outside, Within, or Inbetween? Normativity at Work in Empirical Practical Theological Research." In *Conundrums in Practical Theology,* edited by Bonnie J. Miller-McLemore and Joyce A. Mercer, 134–62. Leiden: Brill, 2016.

———. "Mapping the Landscape of Nordic Research in Ecclesiology and Ethnography: Contributions and Challenges." In *What Really Matters: A Nordic Perspective on Ecclesiology and Ethnography,* edited by Jonas Ideström and Tone Stangeland Kaufman, 15–38. Eugene, OR: Pickwick, 2017.

———, ed. *Mer enn ord* [More than Words]. Oslo: Norwegian IKO-forlaget, forthcoming.

———. *A New Old Spirituality: A Qualitative Study of Clergy Spirituality in the Church of Norway.* PhD diss., Norwegian School of Theology, 2011.

Bibliography

———. "Normativity as Pitfall or Ally? Reflexivity as an Interpretive Resource in Ecclesiological and Ethnographic Research." *Ecclesial Practices. Journal of Ecclesiology and Ethnography* 2 (2015) 91–107.

Kaufman, Tone Stangeland, et al. "Persondimensjonens betydning for prestens profesjonsutøvelse" [The Importance of the Personal Dimension for Professional Pastoral Practice]. *Tidsskrift for Praktisk Teologi* 33 (2016) 45–57.

Kaufman, Tone Stangeland, and Hallvard Olavsson Mosdøl. "More than Words: A Multimodal and Sociomaterial Approach to Understanding the Preaching Event." In *Preaching Promises within the Paradoxes of Life*, Studia Homiletica 11, edited by Johan Cilliers and Len Hansen, 123–33. Stellenbosch: AFRICAN SUN MeDIA, 2018.

Kvale, Steiner, and Svend Brinkmann. *InterViews. En introduction til det kvalitative forskningsvinterview* [An Introduction to the Qualitative Research Interview]. Copenhagen: Hans Reitzels, 1997.

———. *InterViews: Learning the Craft of Qualitative Research Interviewing*. Thousand Oaks, CA: Sage, 2014.

Lave, Jean, and Etienne Wenger. *Situeret læring og andre tekster* [Situated Learning and Other Texts]. Copenhagen: Hans Reitzels, 2004.

———. *Situated Learning. Legitimate Peripheral Participation*. Cambridge: University of Cambridge Press, 1991

Lawrence, C. H. *Medieval Monasticism*. Singapore: Longman, 2001.

Lischer, Richard. "Why I Am Not Persuasive." *Homiletic* 24 (1999) 13–16. http://rhetoric.eserver.org/aristotle/index.html.

Long, Thomas G. "And How Shall They Hear? The Listener in Contemporary Preaching." In *Listening to the Word: Studies in Honor of Fred Craddoc*, edited by Thomas G. Long and Gail O'Day, 167–68. Nashville: Abingdon, 1993.

———. *The Witness of Preaching*. 3rd ed. Louisville: Westminster John Knox, 2016.

Lorensen, Marlene Ringgaard. *Dialogical Preaching: Bakhtin, Otherness and Homiletics*. Göttingen: Vandenhoeck and Ruprecht, 2014.

———. *Preaching as a Carnivalesque Dialogue*. Copenhagen: Copenhagen University Press, 2012.

Lowry, Eugene L. *The Homiletical Plot: The Sermon as Narrative Art Form*. 3rd ed. Nashville: Abingdon, 2000.

Luther, Martin. *D. Martin Luthers Werke: kritische Gesammtausgabe Weimarer Ausgabe*. http://www.lutherdansk.dk/WA/D.%20Martin%20Luthers%20Werke,%20Weimarer%20Ausgabe%20-%20WA.htm.

Mason, Jennifer. *Qualitaive Research*. Thousand Oaks, CA: Sage, 2009.

McClure, John S. *Other-wise Preaching: A Postmodern Ethic for Homiletics*. St. Louis: Chalice, 2001.

———. "Otherwise Thinking—A Blog" 2012. https://johnsmcclure.com/2012/08/.

———. *Preaching Words. 144 Key Terms in Homiletics*. Louisville: Westminster John Knox, 2007.

———. "What I Now Think I Think vis-à-vis Homiletic Theory." Paper presented at the Academy of Homiletics, 2006. http://www.homiletic.org/english/Rhetorical%20Situation%20and%20Aisan%20Theology%20for%20Transformational%20Preaching%202006.pdf.

McClure, John S., et al. *Listening to Listeners: Homiletic Case Studies*. St. Louis: Chalice, 2004.

Appendix

McCroskey, James. *An Introduction to Rhetorical Communication*. Boston: Allyn & Bacon, 1997.
McGrath, Alister. *Christian Theology. An Introduction*. Oxford: Blackwell, 1997
McKinney, Lora-Ellen. *View from the Pew*. Valley Forge: Judson, 2004.
Mikkelsen, Hans Vium, et al. *Liv og konsekvens. Bonhoeffers teologiske arv* [Life and Consequences. The Theological Heritage of Bonhoeffer]. Frederiksberg: Aros Forlag, 2013.
Mulligan, Mary Alice, et al. *Believing in Preaching: What Listeners Hear in Sermons*. St. Louis: Chalice, 2005.
Mulligan, Mary Alice, and Ronald J. Allen. *Make the Word Come Alive: Lessons from Laity*. St. Louis: Chalice, 2005.
Mursell, Gordon, ed. *The Story of Christian Spirituality. Two thousand Years from East to West*. Minneapolis: Fortress, 2001.
Nel, Malan. *Ek is die verskil. Die invloed van persoonlikheid in die prediking* [I am the Difference. The Influence of Personality in Preaching]. Bloemfontein: CLF-Uitgewers, 2001.
Nicol, Martin. *Einander Ins Bild Setzen: Dramaturgische Homiletik* [Put Each Other in the Picture: Dramaturgical Homiletics]. Göttingen: Vandenhoeck und Ruprecht, 2005.
Nielsen, Bent Fleming. *Genopførelser. Ritual, kommunikation og kirke* [Re-enactments. Ritual, Communication and Church]. Frederiksberg: Forlaget Anis, 2004.
———. "Ritualization, the Body and the Church: Reflections on Protestant Mindset and Ritual Process." In *Religion, Ritual, Theatre*, edited by Bent Nielsen et al., 19–45. Frankfurt: Peter Lang, 2009.
"NVivo." http://www.qsrinternational.com/nvivo-product.
Ottoni-Wilhelm, Dawn. "New Hermeneutic, New Homiletic, and New Directions: A U.S.—North American Perspective." *Homiletic* 35 (2010). http://www.homiletic.net/index.php/homiletic/article/viewFile/3388/1600.
Oxford English Dictionary Online. https://www.oed.com/.
Park, H. W., and C. Wepener. "Empirical Research on the Experience of the New Homiletic in South Korea." *Verbum et Ecclesia* 37 (2016) 1–10. http://www.ve.org.za/index.php/VE/article/view/1458/html.
Pearce, Barnett. *Kommunikation og skabelsen af sociale verdener*. [Interpersonal Communication: Making Social Worlds]. Viborg: Dansk Psykologisk Forlag, 2012.
Pearce, Barnett, and Kimberly Pearce. "Taking a Communicative Perspective on Dialogue." In *Dialogue: Theorizing Difference in Communication Studies*, edited by R. Anderson et al., 39–56. Thousand Oaks, CA: Sage, 2003.
Piper, H. C. *Predigtanalysen. Kommunikation und Kommunikationsstörungen in der Predigt* [Sermon Analyses: Communication and Communication Probolems in the Sermon]. Göttingen: Vandenhoech & Ruprecht, 1976.
Pleizier, Theo. *Religious Involvement in Hearing Sermons: A Grounded Theory Study in Empirical Theology and Homiletics*. Delft: Eburon Academic, 2012.
Ralph, Nicholas, et al. "The Methodological Dynamism of Grounded Theory." *The International Journal of Qualitative Methods* 14 (2015) 1–6.
Reid, Robert. "Authenticity in Preaching." Paper presented at the Academy of Homiletics, 2014. https://www.academia.edu/9829217/Authenticity_in_Preaching.
Reid, Robert S. *Slow of Speech and Unclean Lips: Contemporary Images of Preaching*. Eugene, OR: Wipf and Stock, 2010.

Bibliography

Reiter, Keramet, et al. "Denmark doesn't treat its prisoners like prisoners—and it is good for everyone." *Washington Post,* 2016. https://www.washingtonpost.com/posteverything/wp/2016/02/02/denmark-doesnt-treat-its-prisoners-like-prisoners-and-its-good-for-everyone/.

Ricœur, Paul. *Interpretation Theory: Discourse and the Surplus of Meaning.* Fort Worth: Texas Christian University Press, 1976.

Rietvelt, David. "A Survey of the Phenomenological Research of Listening to Preaching." *Homiletic* 38 (2013). http://www.homiletic.net/index.php/homiletic/article/viewFile/3867/1894.

Ryman, Björn Ryman, and Peter Lodberg, eds. *Nordic Folk Churches. A Contemporary Church History.* Grand Rapids: Eerdmans, 2005.

Scharen, Christian B., ed. *Explorations in Ecclesiology and Ethnography.* Studies in Ecclesiology and Ethnography. Grand Rapids: Eerdmans, 2012.

Scharen, Christian B., and Anna Marie Vigen, eds. *Ethnography as Christian Theology and Ethics.* New York: Continuum, 2011.

Scharen, Christian B., and Eileen Campbell-Reed. *Learning Pastoral Imagination: A Five-Year Report on How New Ministers Learn in Practice.* New York: Auburn Theological Seminary, 2016. http://pastoralimagination.com/wp-content/uploads/2016/02/Pastoral-Imagination-Final.pdf.

Schilling, Heinz. *Martin Luther. Rebel i en opbrudstid* [Martin Luther. Rebel in a Time of Change]. Kristeligt Dagblads, 2015.

Schön, Donald. *Den reflekterende praktiker—hordan professionelle tænker når de arbejder.* [The Reflective Practitioner—How Professionals Think When They Work]. Copenhagen: Forlaget Klim, 2001.

Strauss, Anselm, and Juliet M. Corbin. *Basics of Qualitative Research: Techniques and Procedures for Developing Grounded Theory.* Thousand Oaks, CA: Sage, 1998.

Sundberg, Carina: *Här är rymlig plats. Predikoteologier i en komplex verklighet* [Here is Plenty of Space: Preaching Theologies in a Complex Reality]. Karlstad: Karlstad University Studies, 2008.

Sundkvist, Bernice. *En predikan—nio berättelser: en studie i predikoreception* [A Sermon—Nine Stories: A Study in Sermon Reception]. Skrifter i Praktisk Teleogi 45. Åbo: Åbo Akademi, 2003.

Swinton, John, and Harriet Mowat. *Practical Theology and Qualitative Research.* London: SCM, 2006.

Taylor, Barbara Brown. *When God is Silent.* Boston: Cowley, 1998.

Taylor, Charles. *Modernitetens ubehag—Autenticitetens etik* [The Ethics of Authenticity]. Aarhus: Forlaget Philosophia, 2002.

Thøisen, Sanne. *Dialog undervejs. Mundtlighed, retorik og imagination i nyere amerikansk homiletik* [Dialogue along the way. Oral Communication, Rhetoric and Imagination in Recent American Homiletics]. Aarhaus: Aarhus University Press, 2005.

Thorborg, Steen. *Kommunikation—teori og praksis* [Communication: Theory and Practice]. Copenhagen, Hans Reitzels, 2014.

Tutu, Desmond. *Gud har en drøm. En vision om håb for vor tid* [God Has a Dream: A Vision of Hope for Our Time]. Copenhagen: Ascheoug, 2004).

Van der Geest, Hans. *Du hast mich angesprochen—Die Wirkung von Gottesdienst und Predigt* [Presence in the Pulpit: the Impact of Personality in Preaching]. Zurich: Theologisher, 1978.

Appendix

Ward, Pete, ed. *Perspectives on Ecclesiology and Ethnography*. Studies in Ecclesiology and Ethnography. Grand Rapids: Eerdmans, 2012.

Wenger, Etienne. *Praksisfællesskaber. Læring, mening og identitet* [Communities of Pracice: Learning, Meaning, and Identeity]. Copenhagen: Hans Reitzels 2004.

Wigg-Stevenson, Natalie. "From Proclamation to Conversation: Ethnographic Disruptions to Theological Normativity." *Palgrave Communications*. http://www.palgrave-journals.com/palcomms.

———. "Reflexive Theology: A Preliminary Proposal." *Practical Matters* 6 (2013) 1–19.

Williams, Rowan. *Silence and Honey Cakes: The Wisdom of the Desert*. Oxford: Medio Media, 2004.

www.ingramcontent.com/pod-product-compliance
Lightning Source LLC
Chambersburg PA
CBHW050819160426
43192CB00010B/1821